CONVERSATIONS ON EQUITY AND INCLUSION IN PUBLIC TRANSPORTATION

PAUL COMFORT

Print ISBN: 979-8-98554-830-3
eBook ISBN: 979-8-98554-831-0

Published by Comfort Consulting Worldwide, LLC.
Art consultation Sudeep KP
Editing assistance Jenna Comfort

Thanks to the contributors to this book who are committed to providing equity and inclusion in public transportation. Also, thanks to my employer Trapeze Group and Modaxo for their support of this endeavor.

BOOK REVIEWS

"Paul's exploration of diversity, equity, and inclusion as they relate to public transit shares timely and compelling conversations with leaders in the field. As a nation founded on the principles of equality, justice, and liberty, we continue to struggle with delivering on those ideals for all people. For those of us whose starting point on the so-called economic ladder of success was on a low rung, public transit has played a key role in ensuring access to education and employment – in many ways an equalizer. Paul's book helps to inform decision makers about providing equitable transit mobility in an ever-changing environment. As transit leaders we must remain intentional and proactive in our efforts to serve the communities who need us the most."

ALEX WIGGINS
CEO REGIONAL TRANSIT AUTHORITY OF NEW ORLEANS

"The COVID pandemic has upended our daily lives and reminded us how much we take for granted. This crisis has also further exposed inequities in our society, including public transit deficiencies in underserved communities. These difficult problems require intentional and coordinated effort to resolve. Paul's work shows his unique gift to engage transit industry veterans, pioneers and thought leaders alike in challenging but invaluable and mission-oriented conversations. The insights, key trends and lessons that Paul shares provide a blueprint for being clear-eyed around our mission and values and the importance of intentional and sustained effort to promote equity and inclusion."

ROD JONES
HEAD OF AMERICAS, MODAXO
BOARD MEMBER, RAINIER SCHOLARS

Paul Comfort's latest book is an excellent compilation of thoughts from leaders who have public transportation in their "blood" and are now passionately exploring ways on evolving the industry in new directions with a focus on using equity and inclusion as the metrics of the future. Each transit system is seeking to understand the value of their achievements and these leaders are exploring the meaning of words like diversity, inclusion, and equity beyond ideas into meaningful demonstrations of measuring their success. I encourage all who are interested in this journey to read this book and follow their ideas and efforts in making the world of transit more meaningful in the future.

PETER VARGA
PAST AMERICAN PUBLIC TRANSPORTATION ASSOCIATION CHAIR

Book Reviews

"An excellent compilation of interviews of some of today's top transportation leaders. One day in the not so distant future we are going to look back on this period of our history and ask ourselves if we did enough to advocate and push for transportation and racial equity. We can all be agents of change and this book helps."

ALVA CARRASCO
PRESIDENT OF THE BOARD OF DIRECTORS, LATINOS IN TRANSIT

"Paul did a tremendous job highlighting that public transit is far more than mobility, but an integral part of our social, economic, climate, justice and equity goals. The COVID pandemic has exposed inequities in our communities and magnified the essential lifeline service transit provides. Through his interviews with transit leaders, Paul has created a roadmap for a more sustainable, equitable and vibrant future, by detailing industry best practices and underscoring the vital role transit plays in our communities. Sacramento Regional Transit is committed to advancing diversity, equity and inclusion for our employees and the communities we serve, and it is wonderful to read about many transit agencies across the country that share the same goal."

HENRY LI
CEO SACRAMENTO REGIONAL TRANSIT DISTRICT, CA
APTA 2019 BEST TRANSIT CEO OF THE YEAR

See the author's book website for blog posts, merchandise, signed copies and more: www.futureofpublictransportation.com

Read **Paul Comfort**'s other books:

Public Transportation – From the Tom Thumb Railroad to Hyperloop and Beyond
Children's Picture Book – *Amazon #1 Best Seller*

Future of Public Transportation
With contributions from over 40 public transportation leaders, associations and companies *Amazon #1 Best Seller*

Full Throttle – Living Life to Max with No Regrets
Paul and other CEOs tell stories from their careers and lessons learned

All Available on Amazon

TABLE OF CONTENTS

FOREWORD

by Bacarra Sanderson Mauldin

"Diversity is a fact.
Equity is a choice.
Inclusion is an action
Belonging is an outcome."
-Unknown-

Our country is in a period of eerily familiar racial tension and diversity awareness that is complicated and exacerbated by politics, persistent poverty, and the ongoing health pandemic. As public transportation leaders, we have an opportunity to lead and engage our respective communities through our ability to be diverse and inclusive internally and offer service equitability that provides access to life's necessities and pleasures. I often compare public transportation networks to the veins in one's body. Just as the flow of blood gives life to a body, the flow of people breathes life into a community or city.

Paul Comfort keeps a pulse on the public transportation industry as the host of the Transit Unplugged podcast and television show. Through his pursuits, he has interviewed numerous current and former CEOs of Transit Systems and has hosted live CEO Roundtables at conferences helping our industry leadership have their voice heard. With this book he has brought more than 15 years of experience in the government and public sector of the transportation industry and 15 years in the private sector side of our industry to the forefront.

Paul is a life-long leader in the public transportation industry, a friend and thoughtful advisor. His supportive and inclusive nature has been a constant source of support for me and other professionals in the industry for many years. Paul is a master connector of people. In this book, he connects his readers with many diverse perspectives and people. It includes conversations with more than twenty top transit executives discussing what they are currently doing in their agencies. This book is a "must read" for transit agency leaders and staff and it includes commentary on how agencies across the U.S. are implementing equity and inclusion in their transit agencies and systems.

Bacarra Sanderson Mauldin
Chief of Staff
Memphis Area Transit Authority

PREFACE

The Covid pandemic provided transit agencies an inflection point and opportunity to reflect on our core mission. Would our systems and city governments continue to be focused primarily on ridership increases or would they now focus on a more fundamental mission – to provide mobility and access to opportunities for all, with a focus on improved customer service and experience? The American Public Transportation Association (APTA) industry survey in late 2020 showed that transit agencies had already begun making this switch – the results showed they removed "Ridership" as their #1 Key Performance Indicator (KPI) and replaced it with "Customer Service" and then also added in "Access to Mobility Options" as KPI #3 behind "Ridership" which was now at #2.

During the peak of the pandemic transit ridership remained higher on core bus services (around 50% in many cities) providing access to essential jobs, while commuters from the suburbs worked from home. So, most commuter bus and rail services saw their ridership drop to under 10% of pre-pandemic levels. This demonstrated that essential workers, riding core bus services, made up the backbone of not only our economy but also our transit ridership.

The US federal government took note and provided several tranches of unprecedented relief funding to transit agencies and through the adoption of the Bi-Partisan Infrastructure Package and Transportation Reauthorization Act made increased transit operating funding a national priority. Transit agencies and the cities that fund them have largely made the determination to now make service for these essential workers and those often left behind in transit planning a priority. These may include people of color, lower income or elderly passengers.

This book explores this new reality of transit agencies putting the focus back on the rider and improving equity and inclusion (E&I) for all. We examine the new trends of utilizing microtransit as a safety net and agencies adopting a "zero fare" policy. By hearing directly from transit agency Chief Executive Officers (CEO) we find out what practical E&I efforts are currently underway and conduct a deep dive into how many are now making decisions through the "lens" of equity and inclusion.

We start the spotlight on the New Orleans Regional Transit Authority (NORTA) and its Chief Executive Officer, Alex Wiggins, the self-described "Equity Evangelist" who is turning NORTA into an engine of equity and inclusion for his city.

We also hear from other leaders as well in cities like Richmond, Virginia and its GRTC Transit System, headed by glass ceiling breaker, Julie Timm. Richmond as the capital city of the old confederacy has shed its roots to become a new leader in focusing on providing services to the traditionally underserved. Julie explains the details of how and why their system is moving toward staying fare free and focusing their new capital investments on ensuring equity and inclusion in their service modes.

India Birdsong from Cleveland is also a barrier breaker as the first woman GM of the transit system there. She talks about the internal groups at the agency helping empower employees, the importance of new bus routes and assisting people with disabilities.

Former Kansas City Area Transit Authority (KCATA) President and Chief Executive Officer Robbie Makinen, the only blind CEO of a major transit system in North America and the "Father" of the Zero Fare Movement as well as one of the first in America to start a large scale microtransit service, Ride KC Freedom, shares his experiences.

We also hear directly from other transit leaders in the E&I movement like Inez Evans from Indianapolis, Noah Berger near Boston, Adelee LeGrand in Tampa, Brad Miller from Clearwater and Tilly Loughborough from Melbourne, Australia in a Q&A format on what is working and what needs work in their cities and agencies. They provide practical advice on approaches to not only improve equity and inclusion in their agencies but also in the cities they serve. For state and national perspectives we turn to David Kim, Past Secretary of Transportation for the State of California and Veronica Vanterpool, Deputy Administrator of the Federal Transit Administration.

We also speak with the leadership team at the American Public Transportation Association (APTA) on industry wide efforts to promote equity and inclusion and get a historical perspective from industry veteran and APTA Hall of Fame member, Paul Toliver. Then we get a look inside some of the major transit industry suppliers like Jacobs, Proterra, Trapeze, Vontas, TripSpark and Lumenor Consulting, who are working on promoting equity and inclusion in their workforce and services. Finally, my friend and industry leader, Terry White, CEO of Seattle's King County Metro provides the closing summary.

While there are details and amazing efforts that we do not address here, this book brings you the direct words and thoughts from leaders of our industry at a high level on "the why and how" we can and should use our transit agencies to promote equity and inclusion as a core mission of our transit services.

PAUL COMFORT, 2022

PUBLIC TRANSPORTATION INDUSTRY AGENCY LEADERS

CHAPTER 1

ALEX Z. WIGGINS

Chief Executive Officer
Regional Transit Authority of New Orleans

Let's hear from Alex...

Paul Comfort: I'm with Alex Wiggins CEO of the Regional Transit Authority of New Orleans

Alex, tell me some about the recent background on New Orleans and where the city's at right now.

Alex Z. Wiggins: New Orleans is one of the most resilient cities I've ever lived in. You know I'm born and raised here. I moved away in the eighties out to the west coast.

New Orleans actually deals with a lot of extreme weather adversity on a regular basis and now Covid. It is a consistent theme, no matter what is thrown at the city, whether it be Katrina or whether it be Covid, the city always marches forward and the perspective of the residents here is really always to do the very, very best you can in any on any given day and any different situation.

And so New Orleans is like all cities across the country right now recovering from the impact of Covid.

We are working on restoring business, obviously, in our case, restoring transit service, and then the city is beginning to generate the kind of revenue that it does, in order to survive. I think what makes New Orleans unique is a highly resilient a tough workforce, a very well committed workforce that's always focused on bettering the city.

Paul Comfort: Tell me about your personal history and how you got into transit, and what motivates you right now.

Alex Z. Wiggins: You know I got into transit professionally by accident.

My first job in transportation was when I was in high school and I got a summer job with Oceanside Unified school district washing and waxing school buses by hand. This was in the early 80s and to be truthful Paul, I fell in love with buses.

There's just something about the responsibility of maintaining them and what they represent that has always resonated with me. To this very day when I see a nice clean shiny bus, I have a very, very positive feeling.

So that's really where I got my start. I really fell in love with transit after college. I served in the military and after my military service, I took two exams. One was to be a bus driver outside of Fort Lewis, Washington, where I was. The other was the Seattle police department test. Well, the police department called first and so I ended up working in law enforcement. For the first 12 years of my career, but my off-duty job was for King County Metro.

And so, transportation, has always been at the core of what I've been interested in.

Then I decided to change careers after 9/11. There was a very unique opportunity at Sound Transit. They were building a light rail line from the airport to downtown. And they were looking for someone to lead the Community outreach for construction mitigation. And so I jumped at that because I knew everyone in the neighborhood, every one of the business owners and most of the community leaders. It was just a natural fit and so I was hired at Sound Transit initially.

I helped them manage community outreach and then because of my law enforcement background ended up helping to design their law enforcement training program. Then my career in transportation really just opened up.

I ended up working at the Seattle Department of Transportation as the city of Seattle light rail liaison, and so we essentially had a regulatory oversight function of all construction related transportation in city. The mayor hired me to be his light rail liaison and my job there was to mitigate all of those Community impacts associated with building a large capital project.

My job was getting out ahead of challenges relative to access for businesses and residents who may have had issues with construction and resolving them.

I then became the chief of staff at the Department of Transportation and since then I've had a chance to work with some great people.

I was a chief administrative officer at North County transit district in San Diego county and I learned about the bottom line and transit. I believe transit is a service, but we still have a bottom line, and we have to be mindful of our decisions and how they impact our budget.

Then I worked for Grace Crunican as her Chief of Staff. She was recently inducted into the APTA Hall of Fame and she's probably the most demanding and tough boss I've ever had. She actually made me a better professional and without her influence I wouldn't be sitting here today, I can say that with 100% certainty.

Then I went to work at Metro in Chicago and you know wasn't politically suited for Chicago.

Then I was lucky enough to work on the private sector side for a while, on the Denver Eagle P3 project, where we are responsible for building commuter rail lines three different lines and then renovating Union Station in downtown Denver, building a new station at the airport, and of course the commuter rail lines. Then I had a chance to work for Phil Washington at LA Metro, where I headed up our law enforcement emergency management division.

Then this opportunity opened in New Orleans. And, given that I grew up here, I felt that I had a shot at the job and decided to go for it and it's been over two years now. There's nothing more pleasing than providing transit in the community where you grew up so, I'm very happy.

Paul Comfort: What an amazing career story. Did you go to LA when Phil went from Denver or shortly after?

Alex Z. Wiggins: Shortly thereafter. I was part of the first management team that he built after he took over, so I joined him a couple of months after.

Paul Comfort: In the last year or two you've really been talking about looking at everything for a transit agency through the lens of equity and inclusion. So could you tell me what that means to you and define that?

Alex Z. Wiggins: Yeah, absolutely. So with regard to equity we're really looking at removing any barrier to mobility or access to employment, etc, access to education.

Any barrier that's tied to any demographic data, you know your ethnicity, your income, where you grew up etc, and having transit being very purposeful about bridging that gap.

I'll give you an example:

We have communities that are essentially transit deserts and then we have other communities where we have transit service every six minutes.

So as a transit agency it's equally important to us to make sure that that young person, that professional, that single parent, that person going out to their first job has the same access to mobility and same level of mobility as someone who may live in a higher income community that is rich with transit resources. So, we're very intentional about removing those barriers that have had adverse impacts on someone's ability, just to get to work or just to get to school or just get to the grocery store.

And Covid really hammered that lesson home for us because, like a lot of agencies, we saw a drastic reduction ridership and drastic reduction in revenue. But we had a population that still had to get to work, and so we had to be mindful about - Okay, yes, we have to reduce service, but when and where do we reduce service? And how do we ensure that we don't harm folks unnecessarily? It really focused our thinking on how we're going to provide equity with regards to transportation mobility.

Paul Comfort: And what does inclusion mean for you?

Alex Z. Wiggins: Inclusion, you know, making sure that again, everyone has a chance to be at the table, and we are hearing all voices. You know in transit, we love to hear from our fans we love, from those advocacy groups that think we're doing everything correctly.

But it's more important, to hear from voices who don't ordinarily attend Community meetings that don't go online to attend our virtual board meetings and to make sure we go out to them and we hear critical feedback.

Or we hear information that we may have overlooked about how to better serve our Community. So we want to be very intentional about having all of those voices at the table and helping us truly plan and then deliver transit service that meets the community's needs.

Paul Comfort: Can you share some examples of what specifically you are doing to produce more equity and inclusion?

Alex Z. Wiggins: Yeah, one of the things that we started was we actually put together racial and social justice toolkit.

Then we look at every major decision, and this goes well beyond a Title 6 review. But every major decision that affects transit service we looked at the actual neighborhood, looked at demographics, we look at all of those factors that may influence our decision.

And we are intentional about not having an adverse outcome, and so, if we identify a Community that's low income that has low frequency with regard to transit, we're going to make a decision that improves that condition in every case. And to the converse, where we have imbalance, we'll address that too. I'll give you a perfect example - our St. Charles street car essentially travels through the most affluent neighborhood in New Orleans, the Garden District Uptown and travels at a frequency of six minute headways.

Our lowest income community in New Orleans East at one time had headways of an hour. One hour transit service for the lowest income neighborhoods and the highest income neighborhoods every six minutes. So we said, "wait a minute". Not only is that frequency a little bit out of whack, but the ridership demand also isn't even meeting the service that we're putting out. So, through a project called "New Links" we were able to redesign our transit system entirely, looking at those balances and making sure we could implement service where it's most needed, and then adjust service a cut backwards if it's not needed. So again, we try to make sure that everyone in the city has access to education, to employment and we try to serve every neighborhood on every route where it makes sense to do so at headways of 10 to 15 minutes, as opposed to hourly as before.

As to the cost, what we found was, believe it or not, we have not experienced the impact with implementing this in phases. And we have not found an increased cost in service hours because we're transferring from where we had balances and so from areas where we had too much service we're now investing in service hours in areas where we did not have adequate service.

Now we're going to provide more frequent service and these lower income neighborhoods, guess what, they don't have bus stops and shelters. They don't have all of the amenities, that you would find in other neighborhoods, and so our capital costs are certainly going to increase. Because, as we increase the local services necessary, we also need to provide those transit amenities.

We are working to make it easier for our patrons to move around the city, and so our New Links Program is a bus route redesign. In the most simplest way we're rebalancing our system transferring service from areas where we have too much to where it's actually needed to improve mobility for everyone.

Paul Comfort: And those tools in that toolkit you mentioned and that study – where can people find that online if they wanted to get practical help?

Alex Z. Wiggins: On our website.

Paul Comfort: Okay, so you've talked about how moving in this direction changes routes and changes bus stops. What about fares?

Alex Z. Wiggins: Well, you know we are undergoing a fare study right now to determine whether or not our fares are priced at the right point. What our ultimate goal will be is to leverage the unique nature of our streetcar system.

We implemented a new, reduced fare structure in January. We lowered the full monthly fare from $55 to $45, as well as introduced senior and youth fare that are significantly less than half the new full fare. A monthly senior fare is $14; the monthly youth fare is $18. Making these changes has made mobility more affordable for everyone and has also increased our monthly pass sales by 40% in the first few months since implementation.

Paul Comfort: What about on the personnel side? You've recently made some big changes. How are you producing equity inclusion in the employee base of the agency?

Alex Z. Wiggins: We have hired chief diversity equity and inclusion officer that's going to champion both our race and social justice initiatives. We are also one of the original signatories on APTA's new Equity Task Force. We hope to inform industry best practices and model such practices at the RTA.

As well as our internal efforts to ensure equity and inclusion and so right now we're in the process of building that but with regard to our hiring obviously we're looking at bringing all voices to the table and investing. Believe it or not, the barrier that we've identified for a lot of folks is promoting education and training.

And so, for a lot of our longtime employees, we are going to invest in them. Our board just recently just passed a tuition reimbursement policy. Where folks who want to finish or want to pursue educational opportunities, we can now reimburse them up to 90% of their tuition and so I think we're going to take real direct steps like that to ensure that we prepare everyone for success.

Paul Comfort: Finally, can you give us some first practical steps for any transit agency that is interested in using transit to create more equity inclusion? What should they do right at the beginning?

Alex Z. Wiggins: I think the very first thing we should do is intentionally seek out those voices we don't hear from. Seek out those voices that may be critical of how transit is operated in a given community and hear what they have to say.

And that will be an informative step to understand where there may be gaps in service, gaps in customer service.

On other issues related to policing etc, we need to hear from our critics, and I think from that conversation we can then begin to design a system that fills those gaps. I would start there.

And that's actually what we did in New Orleans.

Within my first month I went on a city wide a listening tour, where I literally heard from riders and residents and students and not all of their feedback was positive. But we had to take action there to ensure that we operate a transit system that truly provides mobility for everyone.

CHAPTER 2

INDIA BIRDSONG

General Manager & Chief Executive Officer
Greater Cleveland Regional Transit Authority

Here's What India Has to Say...

India Birdsong: Hi I'm India Birdsong, General Manager and CEO of the Greater Cleveland Regional Transit Authority, otherwise known as GCRTA.

Paul Comfort: Thanks. Please tell us about your transit system itself and the service you provide.

India Birdsong: Sure. I'd be happy to.

So the RTA, as we're known as here was formed in 1975. So we've been around for a while and our mission is really to provide public transit services to about 59 different communities and about 1.2 million residents of Cuyahoga County. We are the only public transit agency in the state of Ohio that has passenger rail.

So we're really proud about that. And we're actually the largest public transit agency in the state of Ohio. We have a lot of different service options, including bus, bus rapid transit, trolley, paratransit, and then also three rail lines. So we have about 2,100 employees. Most of them are unionized, our operators and maintenance staff, for example, through our local Amalgamated Transit Union 18.

And then we also have a transit police force of about 82 officers. We're budgeted for a hundred. So we are hiring and we have the Fraternal Order of Police representing those folks. We also have about 300 administrative staff. We are governed by a 10 member board, which is controlled by the City of Cleveland, the County, and also the mayors and managers association.

So we have a pretty diverse group and we're excited to be part of this conversation.

Paul Comfort: Great. So tell us about what you're doing in the areas of equity and inclusion in your city and why it's important to you.

India Birdsong: So, Paul, that's a great question and we're doing a lot. We actually are really taking a lot of steps to move forward in the areas of diversity, equity and inclusion.

I am actually the first female and the first African-American general manager for our GCRTA. And it's really important that we make sure we reflect the community that we serve. So our workforce has to look like the people that we serve. So what do I mean by that? I mean that we have to make sure we are always cognizant and intentional about the diversification of not only our frontline staff, but also our management and also the programs that we have.

In all areas of the county and the city, we have a lot of different opportunities to enjoy that at GCRTA. A couple of things I'll just mention is that we have recently signed off on the Hispanic Promise. We are actually the first public transit agency in the country to sign off on that. And that's really just a public acknowledgement of making sure that we support the Latin X communities in our hiring procedures and our training.

We also are integrating local. And so we're working with a lot of different local communities and artists underground, or otherwise to be able to beautify our transit stations. We're helping people get their certifications and workforce and job readiness programs and we are partnering with a lot of the community colleges. We're really proud about that.

We're also supporting the health and wellness of Cuyahoga County through our Community to Immunity bus. And that's really a retrofit of a bus that we have. And we basically go out and work with the public health professionals to offer the vaccinations in the fight against COVID-19.

So we're doing a lot of those things. And then of course we have fair number of equity projects to make sure that we're maintaining our ability to offer services to the community, regardless of color, sex, origin, religion, all of that good stuff. And reviewing how we can be better and more competitive in ease of use for our fare collection.

We also have a Baby on Board initiative, which basically fights against infant mortality rates in Cleveland, which are way too high, provides increased access to our system, to new mothers and mothers that are going through pregnancy to make sure that they get to their well-baby visits on time and on schedule through public transit.

Of course, we're working with our lobbyists and advocacy group in Washington, DC and of course at the state Capitol in Columbus, to make sure that we get the funding that's necessary to go ahead and push out these programs. And then of course, to round it out, we want to make sure that we are focusing in on the wellness of our employees.

So we have a lot of different programs through our EAP, in management site visits to all of our districts to make sure that we're communicating with our employees on a daily basis.

Paul Comfort: Okay. Great. Please tell us about what actions you are taking internally at your agency in these areas.

India Birdsong: So Paul, we do a lot of different things in including diversity efforts by committee and also by employee resource groups.

I would like to think that the idea that I kind of embody a different type of general manager, as far as profile, and enable a lot of our leaders that are kind of the unfound gems, diamonds in the rough to be able to find their voice and say, Hey, we need representation in these areas. So, a good example of that is our newest employee resource group, which is coming out like gangbusters called Elevating Women Together (EWT).

And that really was founded by 11 of our tenacious female leaders across the entire agency that banded together and say, Hey, we need to be able to talk about female empowerment at RTA. And so they're doing a lot of great things, including registration for voting campaigns, they're doing wellness and mentoring days. They're doing boutiques visits where you can get low cost affordably priced business attire if you're going out for an interview. They're just doing a lot of great things.

We actually just received word this week that we were the recipient of a DEI award that they had for Employer of the Year through WTS, which is Women In Transit Seminar.

So EWT is basically a great option for a lot of our female employees to be able to increase their creativity and also garner some mentoring relationships at RTA. We also have a new mission statement and a new tagline -"One RTA" you'll hear a lot internally here in Cleveland, just to be able to talk about as we start to really accept and absorb the idea of DEI.

We have a DEI committee at RTA as well, connecting the community as our new mission statement is very simple, but I think it gets to the point. And then we also are trying to put our money where our mouth is. Right? So we have the adaptation of an internal scorecard- a net promoter score. So the net promoter score, in addition to the other scorecards that we are creating, really gives us a comprehensive dataset and lets us know how well we are accepted by the user, our customer, as well as the employee. Do they think that we're invested in their success and then making sure that we're hitting our targets in our 10-year strategic plan?

Paul Comfort: All right thank you. So are you making any changes to service delivery?

India Birdsong: Absolutely. Our service delivery patterns are changing by the day. We actually had completed our service redesign over the summer, which was called Next Gen. And that really happens once in a generation for a lot of transit agencies. So we hadn't done that in over 40 years here at RTA. On the heels of the pandemic it really was important to us because we wanted to make sure that we adjusted our travel patterns to match the business community of the return to work folks. And then also just our regular riders who remained true throughout the last two and a half years. So that's important.

And then we also have a lot of TOD or transit oriented development projects that are coming online. 25 Connects is one that comes to mind that really is rooted in the heart of the Hispanic community here in RTA. And in Cleveland, we have a first mile/last mile connectivity pilot that we are getting ready to launch with two partners in the business community.

And then we also have a recent route adjustment and amenities program for the city of Solon, which for those that are from Cleveland or know Cleveland is about 30 minutes outside of our downtown parts of the city, and really gets to the point of making sure that reverse commute and those individuals who may be working not necessarily in the nucleus of downtown can also have accessibility to public transit.

Paul Comfort: That's great. So what do you see as the end goal when it comes to equity and inclusion? What would it look like if it's done right in your view? What would the transit system in the community look like? And how would the transit system be serving the community to create the optimal state of equity and inclusion?

India Birdsong: So Paul that's a great question as well. What does it look like? It really is about being honest. I think it really is important to make the system accessible, make it equitable, make it fair. And then also make it easy to use when you're talking about payment, having the right type of fare connectivity.

And technology and software is really important, making sure that it's cross-generational. So those folks that are kind of mired in the idea that they can only pay with cash, have to be able to access our system, as well as those phones who you can't tear away, their smartphones. We've gotta be able to have that cross-pollination of acceptance of the service, bringing technology to the community, serving as that kind of gap filler.

When you talk about the technological divide, we address that too. For example, by having Wi-Fi availability throughout our systems, including a lot of our transit waiting environments, our stations, as well as on all of our buses and we also want to make sure that we are part of the economic discussion in Cleveland.

We've got to have a seat at the table when economic development is discussed so working with social services to eradicate things like food deserts and making sure resources are available to those who are most in need, talking about mental health and wellness, making sure that we can get people to those appointments is really important to us and making sure that we don't forget any of our community members while we're in the process, I think is what it would look like.

Paul Comfort: Great. Anything else?

India Birdsong: Just I'm really happy to be here today. And to be part of this publication on behalf of RTA, I would just remind people, don't forget about those that are also not quite on the same plane, as far as ability. We all come from different backgrounds and different modes of communication and abilities and mobility.

So the ADA community is really important. We have a paratransit service as well that we really are excited about. And that has become increasingly more utilized and more robust over the last few years. And we rely heavily on the paratransit operators and customers to make sure that we have an equal playing field when it comes to ADA accessibility.

Also technology to stay ahead of the curve. You want to make sure that you can compete. With the mobility service providers, you want to weave in the e-bikes you want to weave in the scooters, you want to talk about ride share, and in those kinds of things, making sure that public transit is in that conversation, being safe while we do all of those things is important.

And then also be active in the business community so that RTA and other public transit entities are represented as we start to really become an "it" city here in Cleveland. Thank you for your time. Thank you. Appreciate it.

CHAPTER 3

ROBBIE MAKINEN

Past President & Chief Executive Officer
Kansas City Area Transportation Authority

Hear Robbie's Vision....

Robbie Makinen: I'm Robbie. I'm from Kansas City. Born and raised my whole life. I have a beautiful wife. I have two beautiful boys, 16 and 14. I haven't seen their faces since they were eight and six. I haven't seen a sunset or a starry sky or any of that. Every time I put something down, I have to remember where it was, uh, 500 times a day.

I lost my vision about eight years ago.

One time immediately after that, when my oldest son was eight, we were sitting in a grocery store parking lot, mom went in and I heard him back there crying. And I said, "Michael, what's the matter?" He says, "Dad, I feel sorry for you." And then asked, "Is this going to happen to me?"

That is a pivotal moment. That was enough to make you go. Uh, you know what, I'm either going to curl up in a ball here, or I'm going to stand up. I'm either going to be in a boat, anchor or a sail and you need to pick one. So what does this have to do with any of you? What does it have to do with public transit?

I'll tell you it is a big deal. We've all gotten, you know, we all get dealt a bad hand, right? Every once in a while. And it's not matter of, of if it's going to happen. It's a matter of when, but the question is, what are you going to do? What had happened? How are you going to react as an individual in your personal life or as an agency, which we've all seen now, over the past year and a half.

My biggest deal, I guess, is that what you do after that fact makes all the difference in the world? What kind of person are you going to be? What kind of agency are you going to be before I lost my vision? I was that guy. I was ambitious. Right. I wanted a bigger car, a bigger house, a better this, a better that.

Now I don't need any of that. I just need my wife and my kids happy and healthy. Everybody needs to get a dose of perspective. All right. And nobody ever gets it until you get dealt that bad hand, nobody ever gets it until your wife comes home with a lump on her breast, your father gets Alzheimer's, you lose your vision, whatever that is.

What I pray for you here is that you get it ahead of time and that you're able to answer the question. Why, why do I get up in the morning? Why should, why should anybody care? Why do I do what I do? Everybody wants to you meet somebody. Oh, hi. What do you do? I like to ask, why do you do what you do? That's the question.

If you can answer that as a person and answer that as an agency, then as far as I'm concerned, you're headed in the right direction. Our ability to say why - our ability to say we're here to help people. And they're not to us. They're not ridership. They're not customers, they're not with their people. They are members of our community. They're our family. They're our they're part of our city.

They're a part of our lives every day. And if we can change that optic to where you're from somebody pushing a broom all the way to the C-suite that we actually care about the people that we're dealing with. That's going to put us in a much better place. So how do we do that? All right. I'll talk about, uh, I'll talk about zero fare.

ZERO FARE

Four years ago, when I started talking about zero fare, I was talking treason. Everybody says, oh, that can't work. And there'll be, you know, cats living with dogs, safety problems, and, and society will break down as we know it. Well, we've been doing zero fare region wide here for over a year and none of that happened, but it wasn't like we just turned on a light switch.

Okay. It was a strategic methodical plan. To get us to that first, we made transit free for all of our veterans. We've had over 5 million trips. Then we made transit zero fare for all of our Kansas City schools. Okay. Then we went to safety net providers, domestic violence, shelters, folks like that who really needed a hand and we did it there. Right. And what we found out is by allowing those folks to take that money that they used to do to buy passes and whatever, to now put that back into the services. Look, this is about you as a transit agency, not being off on an island by yourself. It's about you weaving yourself into the community fabric.

It's about you becoming a part of the solution, no matter what that is, what you have probably heard me say before is when you plan a transit round trip from A to B and then you put the blinders on, and then we normally say, okay, anything that happens along that corridor? Well, that's somebody else's fault.

That's the community's fault. That's, you know, that's somebody else's deal. It's not in our wheelhouse. We just do public transit. Well, if you take those blinders off and you become a part of the community, then you get put higher up in the waterfall. What I mean by that is then you become a part of the solution.

You become a part of the structure itself. What you and I know is public transit is that one thing that connects everything. Especially during this pandemic, I know all of us can sit around and say, you know what? Because of us, our cities kept breathing and they kept breathing because the people who needed us the most, we were helping get to essential jobs, essential work, essential everything.

TRANSIT'S FOUR PILLARS

So what we're going to do and what we're doing here at Ride KC is concentrating on four pillars, four pillars of public transit, and it's all about access.

ACCESS TO HOUSING, ACCESS TO JOBS, ACCESS TO EDUCATION AND ACCESS TO HEALTHCARE.

So as we redesign our system, we're going to use those templates and those overlays, not only to help that planning process, but then also do it with zero fare.

Now I get it, you know, you say free transit and everybody comes back at me and says it's not free, somebody has to pay for it. But you know, what do you want to invest in? Okay. You want to invest in some more roads that we use, a couple of more lanes we don't need, or do you wanna invest in people, you want to invest in your community by doing that in Kansas City, by us investing in our people and in our community and our friends.

Over the past year, we kept the city breathing. And not just from a service standpoint, if you talk about that zero fare. Yes. If you want to think about it, individually with you, with your agency, then you're going, oh yeah, that's a lot of revenue. I lost a lot of revenue, but if you think about it wholistically as a partnership with your community, with all these providers and with city government, then it's a whole different story.

INVESTING IN YOUR COMMUNITY

So by investing in people, what we've done is we are still doing 30,000 trips a day or better when everybody else's ridership dropped. We never dipped below 60% ridership. And that was with half the service gone. My point is, is that people need us. All right?

And we shouldn't run away from the people that need us the most we should run toward. Okay, 75% of my ridership are people that need us every day. I am not going to run away from them and look for some other shiny thing. We're going to run toward them and we're going to take care of them.

And if you can weave yourself into that community fabric, then people start thinking of you as an agency. Different. Not like you're just out there in the wind. And then all of a sudden, oh yeah, by the way, how are we going to get people somewhere?

Okay. You know, it happens all the time. I say it all the time. Somebody goes out to a green field and they build a big building and hire 1200 or 1600 people. And then a month later they're coming to you going, "our public transit system stinks. We can't get people to work." Why? Because you want to part of the process in the beginning by weaving yourself in the community fabric with your safety net providers, your economic development teams, with your public works folks, all of that. You set the stage for you to be a part of the process, not the afterthought, where they come looking for you later.

And that's what we're doing. And that has made all the difference in the world. We're talking about a $1.50 at a 30,000 rides a day. You're talking about, um, what, you know, do the math. It's millions that the KCATA, the transit authority is pumping right back into the local economy, that money's not leaving.

It's not going to a tax shelter in the Bahamas it's going right back into the local community. It's going to buy a pair of shoes, some prescription, some groceries, whatever that is. Stop thinking about yourself as just a transit agency. Why do you do what you do? Why **to help people, to connect people to opportunities.**

So, if you're going to pump that kind of money back into the economy, that's going to turn it back 10 fold, and we've proven it from ridership.

SAFETY WITH ZERO FARE

Let's talk safety for a second. Well, oh my gosh, you do zero fare. Everything's going to go crazy. Well, a lot of you have done it just because of COVID to help, but we were ahead of the game and we were already doing it. And our crime incident rates went down 35% this year.

Nearly every time, over 80% of the time we ever had an incident on a vehicle, it was over a farebox dispute, which I think is ridiculous. And I think coming up on a $12 million bill that I would have to redo my fare boxes is, is silliness. And then I can invest that money in people. I can invest it in the community and I can get my team around here to be able to focus on the "why" of what we do.

When I put my head on the pillow at night, I know we've done something. I know I've made a difference. I used to have some people come and go, well, you know, we should get a pin or a badge for, uh, for not getting in an accident for, you know, the last year or whatever. I said, that's your job.

What I want to give an award out for is the stories like we had three of our maintenance guys who saw a car. Uh, the lady was slumped over the wheel, ran into a wall. There were kids in the back seat. It started backing up. Our guys jumped out, went and took care of it.

Had another operator who it was two degrees outside and, and she saw a guy at the bus stop without any shoes. Unbelievable. She pulls over, gets him on the bus. She calls dispatch says, Hey, look in our lost and found. Anybody, got a pair of shoes? Dispatch sends a supervisor out and give the guy a pair of shoes.

You know, I got a hundred stories like that. And so do you, my point is those are the rock stars, and those are the people who every day go in knowing that they're going to make a difference in somebody's lives. What I tell anybody here is, if you just come here to make a paycheck, then you're not answering the question why. And you know what? This probably isn't the place for you. Okay. If you want to come here and make a difference. If you can answer the question, why, why do I work here? I tell my people all the time you affect more people's lives, then most people get to do in a lifetime - take advantage of that.

Again, perspective is everything right? And, and I pray that we've all gotten that during COVID here.

ZERO FARE AND ECONOMIC DEVELOPMENT

So, from an economic development standpoint, I'll talk about that for a sec. From a development standpoint, what we're doing in Kansas City is we're trying to put public transit as a part of the incentive process rather than, you know, taking money out for TIF and all that.

And we all lose that money all the time. We're, we're trying to be a part of the process, a part of the solution, which is if you're going to build this thing, part of that clawback has to go to public transit in that area and, or zero fare. So you can show a community benefit someplace else, right over on the East Side, whatever that may be, that's the way to go. Okay. If you can get in those conversations in the state of

Missouri, we get a get a little $300,000 some dollars a year for a line item for public transit. You know, we're, I think we're like 48th in the nation.

And of course that's probably not going to change, but here's what we can do. We can go around and we can talk to people about economic development money. We can talk to people about healthcare. We can talk to people about veterans and we can talk about job access. And when you start having those conversations and that public transit is a piece of that, then you can partner up with those kinds of things, it changes, it changes the whole optic. That's what we're going to do. Okay. And it, and it's working.

Zero fare has been absolutely wonderful, but it's not zero fare just for zero fare's sake. And like I said, it's not just a switch that you flip on. We've been slowly moving in that direction.

ZERO FARE AND HOMELESSNESS

Sometimes I'm asked, how do you handle folks that are homeless? How do you do that? Well, you know what. There, but by the grace of God go all of us, right? So we're not going to treat people different. We're not going to get ourselves or operators in a situation to where they're picking winners or losers.

But here's what we are going to do. All right. Rather than putting an officer with a gun on the bus, what we've done is work with some of our local providers, some of our safety net providers, who now they're their customers, their clients, their people get zero fare transit.

So having some of those homeless agencies actually, when they do their outreach, having them ride a vehicle, to be able to offer resources, to be able to spot situations, to be able to find folks that they want to find too. That kind of partnership is huge. That's innovation.

HUMAN CAPITAL

When it comes to the human capital, when it comes to humankind, that's what we want to do around here. What I always tell people is, from a leadership standpoint, we're doing a great job. But remember it, you know, you as a leader, if you hide behind a rock, your team's going to hide behind a mountain. And that's just a fact.

There's plenty of people on my executive staff that I can't do what they do. They don't do what I do. But our ability to sit around a table and be able to throw some red meat on the table and say, Hey, what about this? Hey, what if we tried that?

So now our folks with disabilities, not only do they ride fixed route service for free, and they get paratransit service for free. Now we also have an on-demand TNC type service that we do in house with a Public Private Partnership. So if you wanted that service, you could get it. And because it's a premium service you would pay.

I guess my point is there is there's room in the tent, and I said this four or five years ago, and everybody thought I was crazy. There's room in the tent for everybody. All right. Because at the end of the day, you're the ones, you're the one that's going to do the most good.

So that we can get folks where they need to go, especially the ones that need us the most. We've got folks losing apartments, losing jobs, losing homes, and their ability to be able to access that region, maybe to find another job. Those four pillars, just like I said, they're fantastic, but they're nothing, unless you wrap them in the foundation of social equity.

And the social equity piece is breaking down barriers so that your folks can get where they need to go. You're opening up opportunities for everybody. Again, saving that $1.50, that's about $1,000 a year, that you can now have to be able to buy lunch, to buy your kids some extra stuff to whatever that may be.

Why can't you be a part of the community and a part of the community solution rather than just sitting back and saying, well transit's my gig. And that's the only thing we're going to do. What we're trying to do now.

ZERO EMISSIONS

Now we're starting a new strategy called zero fare and zero emissions. And that's another strategy that we didn't just turn a switch on.

We've been going that way for a number of years. Now, two thirds of our fleet is CNG. We we've got our first couple of electric buses in now. So moving that direction to where not only are you giving folks the help they need, but now doing it in an environmentally friendly way, it's a big deal.

ROI & THE WHY

So I guess what I would say the most is, and I say this all the time, what do you want to do? Return on investment? That's what everybody wants to talk about, right? Return on investment. Well, the return on investment for empathy, the return on investment for compassion for social equity far outweighs the return on investment for asphalt and concrete.

It just does. So everybody should be able to answer that question. Why, okay. Why do I get up in the morning? Why do I do what I do? Why does our agency do what they do? And if you can, if you can answer that question and start asking it around, it'll change the direction of your agency. I promise you.

Thank you Paul for this opportunity to share what we are doing in Kansas City and the why.

CHAPTER 4

ADELEE LEGRAND

Chief Executive Officer
Hillsboro Transit Authority

Adelee Says....

Adelee LeGrand: The Hillsborough Transit Authority (HART) was created in 1979 to serve as the regional mobility provider in Hillsborough County, serving more than 1.4 million residents in Tampa, Temple Terrace, and parts of unincorporated Hillsborough County. Hillsborough County is the fourth most populated county in Florida, with a total service area of 1,000 square miles, which is almost the size of Rhode Island. HART operates fixed-route local and express bus service, door-to-door paratransit service, flex-route service, and manages the TECO Line Streetcar System. The system is operated and maintained by a team of 800 dedicated employees.

What is unique about HART is the geographic diversity of our service area. We have the pleasure of serving urban, suburban, rural, and waterfront communities. As you can imagine, operating in this diverse geography makes providing efficient and cost-effective public transit service challenging.

Our local funding is generated from a county wide ad valorem tax. These funds are limited and force us to be extremely creative in prioritizing our current resources and plan to introduce future resources. Fortunately, the community recognized that we needed more funding to advance and expand our service. In 2018, the citizens voted and passed a 1% transportation sales surtax, with 45% dedicated to transit. Unfortunately, the surtax was deemed unconstitutional, and the $500,000 collected could not be spent on transportation.

The good news is the county leadership has voted to put another 1% transportation surtax on the ballot in November. Hopefully, this one will pass without any legal challenges.

Paul Comfort: That's great information. One of the concepts that has arisen here in the US especially over the last couple of years, is the importance of using public transportation to achieve policy objectives, not just transport people from A to B, but acknowledging its role as a valuable community resource to do a lot of things.

I mean, in the midst of the pandemic, we were using the buses to transport people to get their vaccines or actually bring the vaccines to them. Some agencies even took their vehicles with Wi-Fi on them out to apartment complexes and allowed school children who were working from home to get a Wi-Fi connection for internet access.

What are the policy objectives that have been important in Tampa? I know you have been utilizing public transit to achieve better equity and inclusion. Can you tell us about that and why that's important?

Adelee LeGrand: I have mixed emotions about this "new" focus on equity. I recognize why we, as an industry, as a nation, and as a global community, are focused on equity at this time. However, in some of these discussions, the focus seems to be on the discussion, acknowledging the issue, but not on changing the behavior. What I mean is, we must develop a culture where we recognize that success depends on the whole's contribution. And then, the recognition that success was achieved as a result of the engagement of the collective.

So, equity, we must have a workforce that is prepared to deliver what is needed today and adept enough to acknowledge the need to be agile enough to respond to disruptions to ensure that we remain relevant.

My concern is that the focus is primarily on the public sector to ensure that there is equity in our agencies in the transit industry. In many cases, the agencies reflect the communities they serve, granted there is always room for improvement, especially in upper management, but progress is being made.

The private sector also has a responsibility to ensure that there is equity in its workforce. They must go beyond committing to a DBE goal and develop a plan to be more reflective of the communities they serve.

My hope is that we take this opportunity to change our culture, respect our colleagues, listen and respond to our community, and build our success strategy around the collective.

Paul Comfort: How about inside your agency? Are you doing anything different as CEO than maybe has been done before to promote more equity and inclusion?

Adelee LeGrand: My goal is to transition HART from a public transit agency to a public mobility company. And that can only happen with an organization that reflects our community.

We are fortunate at HART. Our organization, on all levels, reflects the diversity of our community. This diversity is reflected on the leadership team, middle management, and throughout the organization. The Board of Directors consists of 12 members, seven women, and five men, and they collectively represent the Black, Latinx, White, and LGBTQ communities. This diversity is reflected on the leadership team, middle management, and throughout the organization.

To respond to an ever-changing industry, we need a workforce that is prepared to tackle the challenges of today as well as those that we will face tomorrow. Our focus is ensuring that our staff has access to the resources needed to go from good to great. (Have to recognize COMTO for their focus on Good to Great.)

We have found that partnering with the right organizations, locally and nationally, can provide the needed training support. At HART, we have a strong partnership with the Hillsborough Community College. HCC is one of the largest educational institutions in Florida. They operate out of several campuses in Hillsborough County and provide excellent, accessible training, on the HART transit line.

We also partner with NTI and APTA. Over the last 12 months, APTA has conducted four Peer Reviews for HART and NTI assisted HART in assessing its leadership training needs. This is not an advertisement for these organizations; instead, it acknowledges that the training needed is available. We just need to be intentional about providing the right tools to prepare our workforce to move the organization forward.

Overall, my goal is to transform HART into a public mobility business. To do so, we must have a workforce reflective of the community, experienced, and capable of addressing the known challenges and prepared to address the unknown challenges that we will face.

Paul Comfort: That's excellent. Anything else you want to share on the topic in general?

Adelee LeGrand: It is all about access. The success of our communities depends on our resident's ability to have access to the services available to improve their quality of life. This access is an individual issue as well as a community issue. How we as individuals define the quality of life is personal, but a community defines itself by the amenities, services, and opportunities it provides.

The true test is whether everyone has access to the benefits the community markets to attract and retain residents. Is everyone receiving the benefits that are provided in the community?

Public transit is a mechanism that ensures that there is equity in accessibility. I believe that a successful public transit system is dependent on the ability to complement other modes. In a city like Tampa and many southern cities, there is a reliance on driving your car. To sustain support, those who drive their \cars must view public transit as a community benefit.

The reality is public transit in Hillsborough County, is funded by people who regularly do not ride. Everyone should feel proud when a HART bus goes by. Like supporting a public hospital. You do not want to go to the hospital, but you are happy that your community has a top-ranking trauma center.

The hospital is a community benefit, just like Public Transit.

CHAPTER 5

NOAH BERGER

Administrator and Chief Executive Officer
Merrimack Valley Regional Transit Authority

Noah's Ideas and Actions...

Paul Comfort: First off, why don't you tell us some about yourself a little bit and your agency.

Noah Berger: My love affair with public transportation probably started when I was six years old and I was growing up in New York City. I got the idea to start collecting bus drivers' autographs, because they were my heroes. New York also offered me a firsthand lesson on how transit is closely tied to equity and power. I remember asking my mom why the #1 train slows to a crawl when the train is elevated at 122nd Street in Manhattan, but the #2 train runs at full speed in the Bronx, where my mom had grown up. She explained that residents living around the #1 train's elevated sections had a strong neighborhood association who advocated for the slower trains to keep the noise down, but the Bronx residents did not. To me, this didn't seem fair. The other important lesson I learned in New York was that transit meant freedom and opportunity. As a kid, I went everywhere by bus and subway—giving me access that my suburban peers did not enjoy. And the freedom opened up my world. While I was often told which neighborhoods white kids shouldn't walk through, in my mind at least, this didn't apply to transit and no neighborhood was off limits via bus or subway.

It took me a while to figure out transit was something you could actually do for a living. So my career took me on a rather circuitous route before landing on being a transit professional, including vending at Yankee Stadium, the Central Park Children's Zoo, working in a homeless shelter, graduate work in philosophy, politics, and community organizing.

Like you, my transit career started at the intersection between human service and transportation. I worked for a Community Action agency in Burlington, Vermont, the Champlain Valley Office of Economic Opportunity, which had received an Enterprise Community grant through HUD to fill gaps in the transportation network for residents of the lower income Old North End neighborhood. Along with a community sounding board, our focus was on the practical matter of getting folks to where they needed to go when they needed to get there

We set up a van service that went out to Tafts Corners in Williston, which was then an unserved job center. We also funded later night service to serve second and third shift workers at an industrial park in Winooski and a service sector corridor along Shelburne Road. Incidentally, the Williston service, which we branded as the "Williston Road Runner," was later subsumed by the local transit provider and is now the highest ridership route in the system. We launched a bike share program before there was technology to do it. We just painted donated bikes white and left them at key locations on the sidewalks and people used them.

It really was a multi-purpose agency. And by the way, I had a staff of one, and that was me. So all the office fights, I took home with me—and lost almost all of them! After that, I went back to graduate school to get a better foundation for what I was doing and got my Master's in City Planning from MIT. While at MIT, I was fortunate to work on the Tren Urbano heavy rail project in Puerto Rico, which was under construction at the time. After MIT, I worked as staff to the MBTA Advisory Board in Boston, which has a unique oversight role over the MBTA. It was while at the Advisory Board that I first started working with community groups along the corridor of the Fairmount Commuter Rail Line, which traveled through the inner-city neighborhoods of Dorchester, Mattapan and Hyde Park, mostly without stopping. We advocated that the best way to serve the corridor was to repackage the route *as if* it were a rapid transit line, rebranded as the Indigo Line. While the T has yet to adopt the Indigo Line moniker, they did reduce fares to subway levels, added four infill stations, and increased the frequency and span of service closer to subway levels, all of which we advocated for.

I went on to spend 15 years in the federal government working primarily as the planning director for the Region 1 office of the Federal Transit Administration (FTA). That's where I really got to see firsthand how the sausage is made, how the money flows, and what is prioritized and what isn't. After FTA, I had various stints in the leadership of a number of transit authorities in Connecticut, as well as most recently in Cape Cod.

The bottom line is that I've been spending my whole life thinking about how transit agencies should be run. When the Board for the Merrimack Valley Regional Transit Authority (MVRTA) appointed me to be the next Administrator and CEO this past July, it was time for me to deliver! Perhaps even, to paraphrase the late John Lewis, cause a little good trouble. The MVRTA serves the greater Merrimack River Valley region, which is in the northeast part of Massachusetts. Its central cities are the mill or gateway cities of Lawrence and Haverhill, although the service area extends as far east as Newburyport and Salisbury, which is on the ocean. We also serve more suburban communities like Andover, North Andover and Methuen, as well as some more rural communities. Lawrence stands out in that it is 83% Latino, and has the lowest per capita income of any municipality in Massachusetts. Systemwide, 75% of our ridership is Spanish-speaking. Folks primarily come from the Dominican Republic and Puerto Rico, as well as Guatemala, Panama, Columbia and across Central and South America and the Caribbean. In the best American tradition, our entire region has been defined by immigrants since the nineteenth century, drawn to the mills that sprung up along the Merrimack River. While the origins, cultures and languages may have changed over time, the story is largely the same.

The first thing I did when I took this role was commit to riding every one of our bus routes. I have used my time on the buses to learn about our system by talking to riders, talking to drivers and seeing firsthand what works and what doesn't. I've talked with passengers about routings, service hours, and seating comfort. I've also invited my elected officials to join me on some of these runs. They quickly figured out it's the best way to get a captive audience with your constituents for an hour.

Regardless of their politics, party or ideology, every one of my mayors, state reps and senators came away from riding our buses with a greater appreciation for what public transportation does. One of the state reps who rode with me is a Republican—supposedly Republicans don't like transit, but it went beautifully and I couldn't have scripted it any better. There were these three old ladies on the bus, all over 90. It was one o'clock in the afternoon and one of them was already on her third ride of the day. They talked his ear off, and clearly made an impression on him. He said to me afterwards, "Wow, what would these woman's lives be like if the MVRTA wasn't here?

Remembering my mom's characterization of how strong community advocacy generates results, I've also been taking my team around to meet with community groups—making sure that every group had access to us. One of the things that stood out in the meetings was that we were invisible. We were an afterthought and have been relying on word of mouth for too long—obviously, that only goes so far. In many cases, people didn't know we were there or view us as being for them. Some of it was baked into our image. Like a lot of municipal looking agencies, we operate very boring white buses with a stripe down the middle. We are almost entirely a flag stop system without bus stops, which surprises people.

That might be fine if you're used to the system you're using. But it can be very intimidating to try to wave us down, particularly if you don't know where the bus is going, when it's going to arrive, where you should stand, etc. The lack of stops can be even more intimidating and a barrier to using our system for recent immigrants or people who may not speak English.

I also found that there was a disconnect internally between our staff on the front lines and management. The drivers, many of whom come from the same communities our passengers do, were often very engaged with our riders and frequently had a lot of fabulous ideas, but they were just staying with the drivers.

Paul Comfort: That's very interesting. Please tell me a little bit more about the system.

Noah Berger: We are one of 15 regional transit authorities in Massachusetts, in addition to the MBTA. There are 16 cities and towns in our district, although we also serve the city of Lowell, which centers another RTA, as well as Plaistow NH and we extend to Hampton Beach NH during the summer, with our popular beach run. We also operate a weekday commuter coach bus into Boston. Before COVID, we carried about two million passengers per year. We have 60 fixed route buses—Gilligs, and 25 cutaways for our paratransit van service, as well as six MCI coaches. Right now, we are at about 68 CDL fixed route drivers, although we really need at least 74 to operate our full schedule. On the demand-response side, we have 19 drivers, but need at least 22.

Like a lot of transit agencies, the national driver shortage has challenged our ability to run the schedule our customers want and deserve. In September, I made the uncomfortable decision to temporarily suspend Sunday service in order to stop dropping trips. My team and I viewed this as the best of a bunch of bad options. We felt that as inconvenient as it was to stop running on Sundays, that was preferable to the uncertainty of dropping trips unexpectedly, which leaves passengers waiting for a bus on the side of the road without being able to plan around the disruption. I've committed to our communities that we will restore Sunday service as soon as we get the drivers. Our Lawrence-based service operates at 30-minute headways, while our Haverhill-based service operates at 60-minute headways. We stop running way too soon—7:00PM in Lawrence and 6:00PM in Haverhill, although I'd love to be able to extend our span of service once we grow our workforce.

Paul Comfort: Do you operate yourself or do you contract out?

Noah Berger: We have to contract out, according to our state enabling legislation. The interesting thing is that what contracting out means is interpreted very differently from RTA to RTA. All the law says is that we cannot directly operate buses. While some RTAs have interpreted this to mean they can do everything except drive the buses, MVRTA has historically taken a very narrow view, such that everybody except the administrative staff is contracted out. That said, since we are co-located with our operating contractor here in Haverhill, I treat everybody as if they're my staff, regardless of who actually signs the paycheck!

Of course, much of the rationale behind the contracting requirement is an anachronism now. The RTAs were first established in Massachusetts back in the 70s, and the contracting requirement has added to the law to take care of the mom-and-pop operators that were then the local transit providers at the time, but now no longer exist. It was not really a privatization initiative and there were no national transit management companies back then—no First Transits or MVs.

Paul Comfort: So, tell us about some of the efforts you've been undertaking recently in the area of equity and inclusion.

Noah Berger: As I indicated earlier, one of the things we realized talking to riders and community groups was that we really needed to be more present. We needed to be more visible in the community.

The first step, even before addressing the transit stuff, was to accelerate our outreach. I've taken my team out to meet with community groups, in Lawrence, in Haverhill, all across our service area and hear from real people, whether we play a role in their lives and if not, why not? This can't be a cameo appearance—we keep coming back, making sure that we have established an on-going dialogue. The next step is to implement some of the suggestions people have made—not only does this result in better service, but also convinces them that they are not wasting their time talking to us. Based on this type of exchange, we've already made routing tweaks, added trash barrels, changed bus seating on future orders, or allowed riders to stay on for a return run in order to access the other side of the street without having to negotiate a crosswalk.

In order to further expand our reach, I've been on community access television and the radio—I know you'd appreciate that, Paul! I have a regular slot on a local station here in Haverhill. My on-air presence even includes Telemundo and Spanish language radio, even though I am anything but fluent in Spanish. Luckily, I have a fabulous team including bilingual transit professionals who translate for me—and the funny thing is, it turns out that, from the sound of the translations, I am way more articulate in Spanish than in English! The bottom line is that communication is a team effort—to reach as far and wide as we need to, I rely heavily on my folks, getting the word out, creating a buzz, generating excitement in every language spoken here. It's not because my team and I like to hear our own voices—it's about expanding the reach of our communication.

One particularly high-profile initiative we've undertaken is to go fare free, starting March 1, 2022. During our December Board meeting, my board unanimously took the bold decision to eliminate fares on our entire fixed route service. In many ways, my board viewed their decision as following a compelling path first cleared in Kansas City, Albuquerque, and a few other inspired properties. Restoring transit ridership as a proactive response to the COVID-19 pandemic was no doubt a key motivator. The board was certainly cognizant of and sensitive to the societal arguments, which resonate strongly in our region, given the demographics of our ridership. Since transit fares are a greater financial burden for lower income people and people of color, eliminating fares reduces racial and economic inequity. Environmentally, eliminating fares incentivizes switching from private autos to transit, resulting in reduced greenhouse gas emissions and congestion. More money in the pockets of our riders, freed from having to pay fares, also means that there will be more money to spend at local businesses. However, from my board's perspective, all of these external benefits were secondary to the direct financial benefits here at the MVRTA. It was my job to demonstrate that this was a policy that was sustainable for the agency.

Paul Comfort: Is that a pilot program, or is it something they've made a commitment to?

Noah Berger: They've made a commitment for at least two years and were very clear that it was on me and my staff to collect the data on benefits—ridership increases, operational efficiencies due to reduced dwell times at stops, costs, etc., which would drive future fare policy decisions. That said, while this might be a two-year initiative, we all acknowledged that wherever we end up in March 2024, we were not going to go back to the old model of fareboxes and onboard payments. We are taking the fareboxes out of our vehicles and they are not coming back.

In fact, the need to upgrade our fareboxes was one key motivation for December's vote. Some twelve years ago, Massachusetts RTAs within the orbit of the MBTA's commuter rail network agreed to join the T's CharlieCard fare payment system using Scheidt and Bachmann fareboxes in the interests of interoperability, which was a good thing. The T also agreed to cover most of the back-office work and costs. The problem was that, first, our interests tended to have much less priority than the T's. Then, a couple years ago, the T decided to go in a different direction and abandon Scheidt and Bachmann for what they are calling AFC 2.0 under Cubic.

While that project is well behind schedule, we all know that the same arrangement will not continue. Several RTAs are staying with Scheidt and Bachmann, but since the equipment and supportive infrastructure has gotten quite long in the tooth, doing so requires a new investment in upgraded equipment. For us, staying with the same technology would have required paying just under $200,000 right now, which just didn't make sense.

Paul Comfort: So it's for fixed route and for paratransit as well?

Noah Berger: It's for the fixed route. And then obviously ADA has to be free too, because federal law says that ADA has to be no more than twice the fixed route fare and there is no way that I can do the math where twice zero isn't anything but zero.

We will be collecting fares on our non-ADA Ring and Ride services in our more rural towns and on our commuter bus into Boston. For both of these business lines, we will be transitioning to a fully account-based system, which will be more efficient and work well for the demographic groups that use those services.

Paul Comfort: Let me dig into this a little bit. What was your farebox recovery ratio and how much money in fares are we talking about giving up and how are you going to make that up?

Walk us through the logic string.

Noah Berger: Like a lot of small to midsized systems, our farebox recovery ratio has always been fairly low. Pre-pandemic, it was in the 9% realm. Having said this, I think that farebox recovery ratio gets too much prominence as a performance metric for transit agencies.

It's illustrative to see that the agencies that were hurt the worst during the pandemic were the ones that relied heavily on fares, while the ones that were able to bounce back and be more resilient were ones that had a lower fare recovery, like ours. This makes sense intuitively, given the relatively volatile nature of ridership, which is in many ways dependent on factors outside our control. From a policy perspective, viewing a high fare recovery ratio as a measure of success has the perverse consequence of disincentivizing prioritizing service to groups that, due to federal law or agency policy, would pay lower fares—seniors, people with disabilities, youth, lower income individuals and families. After all, if my goal is to show a high fare recovery ratio, my best approach would be to focus on services that attract mostly riders paying full fare.

I tend to test implications or unintended consequences of policies by looking at how they operate at the extreme. In this spirit, I pose the following thought experiment: let's say our fare policy was that a one-way fare was $20 million. Under this scenario, let's say Jeff Bezos takes one trip from downtown Lawrence to downtown Haverhill and pays full fare and nobody else rides for the rest of the year. We would have an absolutely fabulous fare recovery ratio, but I would argue a lousy system.

Paul Comfort: I've always said it's like the tail wagging the dog, you know? It's just, it's a lot of effort for very little return.

So how much money are we talking about in a year that you were bringing in and that you will have to then make up?

Noah Berger: Pre-pandemic, we were looking at about $3 million per year. But last year it was less than $600,000. Keep in mind too that we will also see some savings due to the very high cost of collecting fares, as you've noted. While some of the savings will not be realized overnight, we will see savings associated with shedding all those things that go into collecting fares. And this is not an insignificant amount.

This is another part of the economic analysis that really floors people—I know my board took this to heart. We did an in-depth review of the true fully-allocated cost of collecting fares and found that for every dollar we collect at the farebox, we really only see 23.9 cents. Costs examined in this calculation include the cost of the money room, which anybody working in a transit property will tell you is a disaster in terms of staff time and security, the cost of hiring an armored car, vaulting, the fare collection equipment which we've already talked about, as well as the dwell time cost of riders queuing up to pay their fares, which slows the bus route down. If nothing else, I know my staff are pretty excited about shutting down the money room!

Quite frankly, if we didn't collect fares and someone proposed that we start, the fiscally conservative thing to do would be to ask whether what was proposed is an efficient way to generate revenue. As we've seen, it turns out to be a very clunky and inefficient means of generating revenue that comes at the cost of providing optimal transit service to our customers.

Paul Comfort: So you were collecting $600,000 and you're only seeing a quarter of that after expenses. You're talking about having to make up what, something like $150,000?

Noah Berger: That's right. if we're taking our experience during the pandemic as baseline, that's absolutely correct. Obviously once we get back to where we want to be in terms of ridership, those numbers will change and some might argue that we would be leaving more fare revenue on the table. However, part of how we get to our targeted post-COVID ridership is by winning riders to our system due in part to the free fares, so we have to be careful how we estimate true lost revenue.

The question I keep getting, and it's a very legitimate one, is: What are you going to do in two years and one day? That is, after the two-year initiative authorized by my board. I will no doubt need to find new ways to generate revenue. That said, recouping lost fares is only a tiny part of transit's need for more revenue. Regardless of fare policy, I will need to keep up with dramatically rising fuel costs and driver wages that are escalating at a far greater clip than other segments of the economy. We will also need funding to grow service in order to operate the frequency and span of service this area needs and deserves, and this will be true no matter the fare we do or do not charge our riders.

To get there, I will be looking to my friends in the state legislature (there's a reason why I have invited my state reps and senators to ride the bus with me!), the Governor, philanthropic groups, and area businesses we serve. As an example, I just had a meeting with Amazon about what it would take to launch new service along the Route 125 corridor between Lawrence, North Andover and Haverhill that would serve a new warehouse facility they are building. Stay tuned for that one.

In this area, going fare free is actually part of the solution, as doing so will both increase ridership and reduce trip time because dwell time at stops will be reduced. This will allow me to run more service for the same hourly costs. Since both ridership and revenue vehicle miles are key factors in determining our FTA formula funding apportionments, our federal funding will go up. Looking inside the black box, for every additional mile we put on the road, we generate just over 50 cents in funding, based on FY2021 figures, which can add up over the course of a year. Finally, I'm not afraid to look at generating advertising revenue on bus shelters we hope to install as part of a campaign to introduce bus stops.

Paul Comfort: So let's talk a little bit more about fare free and the decision tree process you went through. What your budget is, how it's made up, how you're funded, who your board members are, and was this something you proposed or they proposed, or a meeting of the minds, walk us through that whole process please.

Noah Berger: Our operating budget is about $20 million. As we discussed, fares are a small piece of that. The bulk of our funding comes from FTA and the state, with a lesser amount coming from the local assessments from our 16 member communities, and a limited amount of non-fare revenue from advertising and parking.

When I came here, there was a fairly parochial approach to local funding whereby each city and town was told that they choose the level of service they want and pay for it. While this might sound good at first blush if you believe in local control, it actually gets in the way of the true regional thinking that's needed for robust regional transit. This has been referred to somewhat pejoratively as the "vending machine model of funding transit." I want to get away from this approach and bring a more regional perspective to both service and funding. Certainly, the communities understand that people who live in Lawrence might work in Haverhill, or that people who live in Newburyport might want to visit a friend who lives in Salisbury, etc. We just need to fund and operate service accordingly.

This approach is supported by how real people think. While those of us in local government know exactly where the municipal boundaries are, regular riders really could care less where the town lines are. Part of instituting this approach is disabusing my municipalities of the idea that every time I throw some idea out there, I'm immediately going for their wallets. After all, people tend to be much more creative and experimental if they don't have to pay for it. And of course, the reality is that local assessments, for all the obstacles they've presented to vision and growth, are really a small percentage of the budget.

That said, when local governments are inclined to be experimental and visionary, the city-by-city approach can sometimes allow for the demonstration of locally-driven priorities which can later be exported to the entire region. This was in fact the historical path that helped spur our systemwide free fare initiative. In this way, going fare free in March stands on the shoulders of giants that started locally just in the city of Lawrence before I was here.

Former Mayor Danny Rivera, who was also our board chair for seven years, convinced his City Council to pay the fares for all riders on three MVRTA bus routes that operate almost exclusively in Lawrence—the 34, 37 and 85. Starting in September of 2019, no fares were collected on these routes, with the city footing the bill. While the initiative didn't really have a lot of time to build up momentum before the pandemic hit, we did show ridership increases of 25% to 50%. With the city taking the risk, the initiative also helped mainstream the idea of free transit regionally. Not only did the world not come to end, folks who might otherwise have been skeptical began to say, hey, maybe this isn't as crazy as it first seemed. This certainly made it easier for me and the board to apply the model to the entire region later on. And by making it systemwide, we opened up additional savings that we weren't able to achieve with just the three Lawrence routes. After all, prior to going fare free systemwide, buses on the three routes still kept their fareboxes, which cost $35 thousand a pop; we still had to keep our money room open; we still had to pay people to carry out fare collection across our service.

The other big factor that allowed us to move forward was the availability of federal recovery funds, which are 100% federal funding, and cover operations. Since FTA pays for the net cost of service, which are operating costs minus fares, it is a straightforward calculation to submit for reimbursement after going fare free, since that will just be our operating costs minus zero if no fares are collected. In this way, it's actually much easier than people think, since we do not need to project lost fare revenue—rather, we just get reimbursement for a larger share of our operating costs. While recovery funds are certainly not a bottomless pit of money, it does buy us flexibility and time to identify future revenue streams that would be more efficient, sustainable and lucrative.

In addition to the need for fiscal support, it was on me to demonstrate to my board that I was not asking them to do anything reckless—that taking this step was not a leap of blind faith. Before the board took the vote, I reached out to all sixteen of my board members, who are the designees of each municipality in my district, and went over what we were proposing, what the implications were and who was supporting it.

I tried to meet each city and town where they were and address any concerns. As it happened. I had been on a local cable access show with the mayor of Methuen a little while earlier. The mayor is a proud businessman who came to City Hall from outside politics and bristles whenever someone refers to him as a politician. On the show, he asked me without prompting, "So, it seems to me, if your ridership is down because of the pandemic, why don't you just offer free rides?," adding that "That's from a business perspective. That just makes sense." I filed that away and later took the opportunity to remind my Methuen board rep what her mayor had said on the show. She actually went back and looked at the tape just to make sure. In casting her vote at our board meeting, she referenced the words of her mayor.

Finally, I invited a well-regarded researcher with the Massachusetts Budget and Policy Center who had done a lot of independent work on the benefits of free transit to present at our board meeting. This helped demonstrate that this wasn't just me and my staff, it wasn't just activists and local transit advocates that were pushing this—it was supported by research, which gave my board confidence that this was indeed the right thing to do and prudent policy.

Paul Comfort: It seems like a combination of events occurred. You had the farebox continuation decision point coming up, you had kind of a pilot program started by the city of Lawrence and the Mayor who had the idea.

Then you had the ARPA funds (federal relief funds) coming through, which could help kind of fill that gap for a while. So would you say it was a confluence of events that led to this decision to go fare free?

Noah Berger: Yes, in many ways it was and is the perfect storm. And I do think we are also an ideal proving ground for a free fare initiative due to the compelling backdrop of the area we serve. While my board was motivated first and foremost by our fiscal situation, the outside world and media needs to see the human interest component. While there's a lot of economic diversity in my service district, there's a concentration of poverty that drive the point home for folks swayed by the societal benefits of going fare free. While our fare is relatively low, it's a buck and a quarter, people on that end of the income spectrum will choose not to ride to save that dollar and a quarter. Sometimes it's a choice between access or food; access or medicine; access or being an active, social human being.

Paul Comfort: Are you hearing from any critics going fare free? In some cities, critics are concerned about mental health issues and homelessness being transferred to transit. Have you heard from any critics saying that? And what's your response to that?

Noah Berger: I have heard that—but homelessness is a problem regardless of our fare policy. We get complaints now, valid and otherwise, about homeless people in our bus stations, homeless people in the bathrooms in our facilities. The reality is that no transit provider is equipped to address homelessness and we should not be treating people who are homeless differently than anybody else. We should, however, have behavior-based policies. We should never kick someone off the bus because we suspect they are homeless—we should kick someone off if they are disruptive or disturbing other passengers, regardless of their housing situation. I'm a firm believer that one of the great things about public transportation is that your reason for riding ain't nobody's business but your own. If you want to ride to the end of the line and stay on for the return trip, that's fine by me. I've done that myself on numerous occasions—call it a busman's holiday! If you're riding to get out of the cold, that's fine—so long as you're not disruptive. We should also work collaboratively with human service providers that are better equipped to work with people who may be homeless to make sure they have access to the supports they need and that the right people are addressing the right problems.

Paul Comfort: Anything else on fare free you want to talk about before we go into other topics?

Noah Berger: There are people who have the mindset that even if it may not be cost-effective to collect fares, it is the fair thing to do. This is the mentality that says "If you don't pay the freight, you don't get shipped."

We are trying to make sure that people understand we can actually provide a better service by going fare free. People are used to other things that are fare free like libraries, trash receptacles, parks, etc. These are all public goods that we want people to use. Similarly, transit is a public good that we want people to use, so why wouldn't we want to make it free if we can?

The other question I hear is: What is the opportunity cost of going fare free? Wouldn't it be preferable, the argument goes, to increase frequencies or run later into the evening, or serve more places? My answer is that I would love to do all that—the problem is that I can't make the service improvements on the same time-table that I can change fare policy. Due to the current driver shortage, I am having a difficult time running the current schedule, let alone running later. I am not running Sundays, not because I don't have the funding, but because I don't have the bodies behind the wheel. I don't have the vehicles or space to store them to run greater frequencies right now. While I am optimistic that we will get to a better place regarding our workforce, equipment and infrastructure, we are not there right now—and in fact a good way to make the case for getting there is demonstrating success with our fare free initiative.

OTHER ACTIVITIES -

Paul Comfort: That's good. That's excellent. Now, what else are you doing? You have some fun things with pianos and the café space. Tell me about that.

Noah Berger: That's right—MVRTA owns the McGovern Transportation Center in Lawrence, which is an intermodal hub that serves both MBTA commuter trains into Boston and some of our local bus routes. There is a long-abandoned cafe there that people with long memories remember used to be a coffee shop. It never really made money and has been mothballed for the last ten years or so. Now we use it to store detergent, mops and toilet paper—not exactly a welcoming presence.

So I said, all right, let's activate that space, without worrying about making money or having to put out an RFP requiring us to take the highest bid, regardless of how it benefits the area. We elected to turn the site into a kind of entrepreneurial training center, or incubator space. We're bringing in a local, Latina natural nail artist who will soon set up shop in the former café space. We coordinated with local non-profits that will help her develop a business plan and learn to be an effective businessperson. Meanwhile, she's committed to brighten up the whole area with color, light, and invite other artists to cover much of the concrete with attractive murals, reflective of the greater community. In the courtyard outside the station, we are inviting food trucks in to further enliven the space.

The pianos were pure happenstance. One of my state reps, who has been a big supporter and has ridden the bus with me publicly on multiple occasions, alerted me that one of her kid's art teachers in their North Andover middle school was part of a project to paint pianos in another community. That installation only lasted for the summer, after which the pianos were to be disposed of, which my rep felt badly about. When she asked me "Hey, can you use these pianos?" I said, "This is exactly the kind of whimsy, joy, color that we're trying to bring to our service right now!" We were able to get four painted pianos free and install them in the McGovern waiting areas. They're not always 100% in tune, but they are guaranteed to make people smile. I've gotten a lot of positive feedback about them from community members. We were able to add them right away and give people a sort of preview of coming attractions—they give people a taste of what we're talking about now when we say we're going to add color and whimsey and joy to our buses and facilities, setting the tone for how we want to enhance the whole feel of our system.

The larger initiative to add vibrancy to our system, as demonstrated by the pianos, comes out of the need to be more visible and present in our communities that we talked about earlier. I keep telling people that we don't want to just win back the riders we lost during the pandemic, we want to grab those passengers who weren't riding with us before. In this vein, we're going through a rebranding exercise to better establish our relationship with the communities we serve. Simply put, we can't attract new riders if they can't see us.

We want our name and logo to be welcoming and encouraging. MVRTA doesn't exactly roll off the tongue. We are rebranding our system as hip, fun and convenient. We'll introduce a new name that works well in Spanish, and create a spicier logo. We're going to paint our plain white municipal-looking buses bright colors that will be more visible—in your face if you will—and better reflect the multicultural communities we travel through, particularly the Caribbean islands or Central and South America, where people are used to seeing brightly colored houses and buses. A Lawrence resident originally from Panama City fondly recalled colorful buses there that were affectionately known as "Diablo Rojos" or red devils.

It is important that the new brand comes from the community—that they see it as theirs. We've put together a group of local artists and community members who are going to look at various different options and make a selection that they see as best reflecting our area and people. We hope to be able to roll the new look out at the same time that we launch our fare free initiative, in order to really maximize that splash.

Of course we have to match the imaging up with quality service, but I see getting to where we need to be in terms of quality as being tied to successfully being reflective of and visible to our community. Part of this effort also encompasses actually putting in bus stops with attractive shelters and benches so that people feel more confident and comfortable waiting for the bus.

Paul Comfort: That's great. I've had the opportunity to play pianos in public transit centers all over the world in places like Glasgow, Scotland to Baltimore, Maryland. That's wonderful. Anything else you want to tell me?

Noah Berger: Well, we'll have to get you up here to play our pianos Paul!

One important point I want to make is that it's just as important to apply equity and inclusion internally as it is externally. We've talked a little earlier about the importance of making sure that our outreach, our branding, makes sense in Spanish. As we've discussed, 75% of our ridership and 83% of the city of Lawrence are Spanish speaking. We need to meet our community, our riders, where they are, in their own language. By the same token, we can't be oblivious to the fact that our workforce is drawn from the same community as our riders. Sensitive to this, we recently changed how we solicit drivers by taking out a line stating that drivers had to be fluent in English.

Not only was this practice keeping us from hiring people who would have been great drivers, we actually found that since people have different subjective self-assessments of their fluency, we were excluding the most self-critical, insightful and eager to grow individuals—in short, people likely to make the best employees. Interestingly, this tended to break down along gender lines, as women were more likely to be self-critical of their fluency and take themselves out of the running before they even came in for an interview than men were. It is not in our best interests to deny employment to someone just because they might have a hard time self-identifying as fluent in English, but really could do the job. And by the way, they would probably be better than someone who doesn't speak Spanish in communicating with our passengers, which is another very important part of the job of being a bus driver. While this may seem like a small thing, it sends an important message and helps us develop a workforce that is more reflective of and looks like the communities we serve.

Finally, in prioritizing the connection between our drivers and our riders in every language, MVRTA is better positioned to address shortcomings that we might otherwise not have been aware of. We recently constituted a "Good Ideas Group," or GIG, where drivers have an opportunity to suggest improvements that they know about from serving on the front lines, but may not have felt like they could to bring to management's attention previously. This means empowering our employees at all levels of the operation that their ideas have value and will be taken seriously.

The bottom line is that I am so excited about what we are doing here in the Merrimack Valley—working with the community, our drivers, and other stakeholders. We have so much potential to really make a difference. And the key really is involving everybody—the epitome of equity and inclusion. Come back in a year and we can look forward to showing off some of the results!

CHAPTER 6

JULIE TIMM

Chief Executive Officer
Greater Richmond Transit Company

Listen to Julie...

Paul Comfort: Hello Julie. Can you tell us what's your vision, what's your goal, when it comes to equity inclusion, and what are some of the practical steps that you're taking?

Julie Timm: So, you know, I was talking to these students and they were between 20, 30, 40, 50 years old, leaders across the state who are looking to have more involvement in business or social or other elected official politics.

And they were asking about transportation. So I took them on this a little bit of a journey, asking them about their definition of prosperity, so we're all on the same page. Mobility, of course, we're all interested in mobility and this term of mobility is not just about physical movement, but also socioeconomic movement, which is when we think about prosperity and transportation, physical movement, it's all tied together.

And so if we start with the foundation that the prosperity and the welfare of our community has to do with the strength of our communities, the prosperity has to do with their opportunities, that social and economic connection. And in order to have that prosperity and that community and that social cohesion who actually have the socioeconomic mobility, you have to have that physical mobility to have jobs and healthcare and food and education.

And if you don't have those, you don't have a true opportunity for prosperity. So that's kind of the foundation from which we look at transit. And we look for transit doing exactly that, connecting people from home to jobs, either because they don't have available transportation or because they choose to have a different form of transportation, maybe for social reasons or environmental issues.

And that's where we kind of have our foundation is to understand this. So transit isn't just for other people. It's actually a fundamental and essential core service that makes our region prosperous. So we kind of have to buy into this concept first, in order to buy into why transit should be equitable and not just, you know, something where we just put out a little bit of lifeline service and forget about it. And then not only that, what makes our own transportation experience equitable or useful is that we have the service we've known we needed to have equal access, but it's reliable, it's safe, it's convenient. All those things that we get in our car, we should also be able to have something similar in transit. Okay. So that's the background about equity and prosperity.

Paul Comfort: Tell me about your service area and the background of the city of Richmond.

Julie Timm: Yeah, absolutely. And so you're going to love where I'm going next. Richmond of course, is a region that has multiple counties, 6, 7, 8 counties and cities, about 1.3 million people, predominantly our services are covers about 75% with about a quarter of Henrico County and some in Chesterfield County. The whole region's looking for more. We have a local bus, commuter bus and we started Bus Rapid Transit (BRT) in 2018. This, when across the country, there were the double digit drops in ridership and Richmond launched the BRT, the Pulse, and they did a system redesign that resulted in double digit growth that continued right up into COVID. And with that growth, that's a surprising amount of success.

They went into getting regional dedicated funding from the central Virginia Transportation Authority to put more frequency and more connectivity and more routes in service, looking to start that planning. Now of course, COVID put a change on that, but that's the foundation that I got here with in 2019. It was this idea of transit becoming a more critical part of the economic and social development.

There's a history of Richmond - we're coming up on 400 years. In this region, there's a lot of history that has to do with the slave trade and the Confederacy. And so that's, that's still unfortunately, a very strong component of the history here that hasn't healed fully.

Paul Comfort: Yeah. Richmond was the capital of the Confederacy, right?

Julie Timm: It is. And there's a book. My board chair actually wrote a book about the unhealed history of Richmond.

As to the BRT, it traditionally has connected the business community. And there was controversy before I got here that it was meant just for "rich office people". Okay, and so when you look at it and you look at that design, you can see it. It's a nice looking BRT.

There's some dedicated lanes, level boarding, off board fare payment. You know, and it's separated. It's a nice looking system that was well done. Yeah. It'd been better if they would have put full dedicated lanes, but there was a lot of feelings that this was done only for the businesses and it kind of ignored everyone else. You really have to look at the fact that system was redesigned as well to connect into it. There was a Title 6 complaint filed with the FTA, when this was put in place.

Some of the areas over on the east end actually received less service and it was harder to connect as the system was redesigned to kind of focus, to connect to it from the pulse of the region. It was before I got here and I hate to criticize something that I have second hand or third hand knowledge of. Yeah.

So when we looked at that, and then of course the discussion about how it had this whole economic value. Look, when The Pulse hit in 2018, we did start seeing this high growth that started to increase pretty quickly, where before it was kind of just starting to look like it was stabling out. So, you know, you could extrapolate that the growth would be less without The Pulse and more with The Pulse.

Regardless there was that increase in value. And we see from people, businesses and homeowners along the corridor that the property values are increasing dramatically. Okay. And this is where I start to take a turn. Yes. Because so much has been focused around this, the BRT and the wealth from the BRT.

With the route redesign, with the growth we were looking at, we were in the close to 9 million annual trips, pre COVID projecting on to be hit crossing that 10 million threshold. So pre COVID, this is where we were looking. We were looking to growing our non-work base, but we were still work-based and then COVID hit.

And I started looking at the data completely. And this is where we start looking at equity. I'm looking at the BRT here. And this concept that constantly came up was in order to get more money for our local bus routes you need to invest in the premium service because it'll flow over into the rest of the local bus. If you want to make local bus equitable, invest in the premium service, the BRT and the light rail, and that will get the non bus people to see it feels like they can own it. They'll participate in it, and then you can flow through to really make it.

And that's why you see a lot of BRT commercials being very much more affluent base. When COVID hit, I really started looking at our data based on mode, as opposed to how usually I would look at it based on overall ridership. And then I broke it down by mode and it was striking how everyone else is when they talk across the country, that up to 93% of bus ridership stopped.

And I'm like, no, it didn't. Well, yeah, it did on express routes because they were teleworking. And then we looked at how much of our service was express. It's tiny. Even BRT which is relatively new, it was a growing a significant part of our service, nothing to sneeze at, but we still had the majority of our service on local bus.

And when it dropped after the Covid pandemic hit, it only dropped by 22%. You've heard me talk about these things. Looking at July of 2019, July of 2020 and July of 2021 it shows we are back to pre COVID levels on bus service. BRT is coming back and local bus ridership levels are back to normal.

And this is where all I started thinking. Okay, when I look at who our bus riders are, they're predominantly low income households. Predominantly people of color, predominantly people who were buying passes with a one-day pass or the cash fare. Look at where they were coming from and where they were going to predominantly, still riding coming from economically distressed areas.

What that does is, it paints a picture that bus ridership is essentially low-income black people. Now, local bus is essential workforce. You know, these are the people that support our economy and supported us during the pandemic.

When so many people got to stay home, these are the people that continued to work at pharmacies, who continued to get the drugs out to people who had diabetes. These are people who continued to go and stock our shelves with toilet paper when toilet paper couldn't be had. These are people who washed the dishes so the rest of us could stay home and get door dash, delivered food to our door, and they cooked that food.

They continued to work because those jobs can't be outsourced to your house and they kept riding our bus service.

When you make transit, when you break down the barriers of transit and that's, what I've been trying to do is break down the barriers of transit. And as I break down, those barriers, those social issues are creeping more and more onto transit and making them transit issues. They are not transit issues to be clear, like homelessness, joblessness, health care, mental health care - these are not transit issues. But when you make transit more accessible and more affordable and you take down the barriers of transit, it becomes more accessible to people who are vulnerable. And then the fear is, is that if we highlight or shine a light on these elements, we will lose the ridership that are more choice because they don't want to actively engage in these very real community social issues.

When you look at our service you can see the under investment we have in areas that keeps people with a lack of shade at bus stops, the lack of sidewalks etc..

On requests for stops to some new social services, we checked to make sure they were on a transit line, but the transit line stop area doesn't have sidewalks, doesn't have shelters and is hourly service. That is Monday through Friday, during peak times when a lot of people in the housing have to work night shifts. So people aren't considering the placement of essential services, social services or voter services, where they look at transit.

All of these are community issues, but they transfer themselves over on the transit when transit becomes for "other people". I love this quote from Henry Ford. "You always do what you've always done. You'll always get what you've always got."

So we're actively going to try to invest millions of dollars of better infrastructure for people, including the sidewalks. I mean there's the connectivity and the site. We can get better sewer and drainage. We can get better sidewalks and connectivity so that people have a place. And we just have to make that investment. It's hard and it's super expensive because transit typically pays for the shelter. So I'm working to try and get my partners to get that sidewalk money.

We can do things that are multimodal, that attract everyone that serve all means, but we have to envision it to create it. And we have to look at frequencies and connections and the funding, and how do we make it to that? So someone's not on the bus for three hours to get to work with multiple transfers, but they have more reasonable connectivity and they have more ability to use multimodal to get into that framework.

And it's mental health job to deal with the homeless and it's social services and the housing to deal with housing. But if we connect with them, it's no longer a transit issue, but it's also not a homeless or mental health issue anymore because now she's a person being cared for because we reached out.

We're working to put those frequencies in place, but also to reach out to the city and other places so that passengers have a place for childcare as a single dad, so that he can put the hours in the work and get the money to take care of his son.

And if we have the will to, even though it's hard and it's a huge burden, if we lift it together, we can make a difference.

And then I end with this, you know, remembering what prosperity really means. It's why is it important to understand those definitions and to understand. Well, I'm only responsible as a transit CEO for putting my buses on the street. I am responsible as a human and a member of the community for all of this.

Paul Comfort: That's great, Julie,

So the practical things that you're doing, that I can see are improved bus shelters, trying to improve the frequency of some service?

Julie Timm: There's some discussion about looking at this idea about 15 minute city. Being able to get anywhere from one side, to the other in 15 minutes. That means if you're going to have a 15 minute city, you have to be looking at the core network being 10 minutes or better headways.

Right? Get on and get there. So there are conversations that are being had with people about what would it take to get to be a 15 minute city? I gave some initial cost quotes and they all kind of freaked out. There's no way we can afford that. Yeah. But the fact is the conversation starting is the first step to getting to a 15 minute city.

And what that connected to me looks like.

Paul Comfort: So shelters, sidewalks, headways, what other kinds of proposals and what about fares?

Julie Timm: We have approval for zero fares. As long as we have the federal money supporting us, we are looking at a state program, a department of rail and public transportation.

The state has a pilot program where they can help regions wean into it by having a high amount of state subsidy to low over three years, but it requires a local match. And while I have the city of Richmond committed to zero fares, I don't have the money for a local match.

We will continue on if they don't. The next phase is to do the study, to go into fare capping, account-based. So that we can get into fare subsidies for low income. Now that's a great system, but it is a more expensive system. It still creates barriers to some people who can't get those cards.

If you can't go to zero fare, it's the next best thing, but it is more expensive and it does still maintain a lot of barriers to transit that you don't get when you go to zero fare.

Paul Comfort: What about micro transit? Are you doing anything there?

Julie Timm: Yes, we actually are doing a study right now. It's a multi-phased study. The Department of Public Transportation in Virginia has one of the actual active pilots for micro transit. We have a study that's starting right now to work with all of our municipalities to identify their needs because all of them would like to have something, but they don't all want or need a 40 foot bus.

Clearly there's areas we have that are rural, that a 40 foot bus just doesn't make. But some kind of a senior ride or On demand model would help. We are doing the study and to be able to understand what and where those needs are. So that's our first phase is help our jurisdictions who are more suburban, rural, do the study to identify the needs, the populations that need it, the resources they need to get to what other kinds of funding is available to make those connections. And can we, as an agency provide that service or can we provide pass through grants for nonprofits or other smaller organizations to provide those services that give people that are either connected to transit or in areas where they're so far out. At least they connect to health or to food or other things. And you see those popping up across the state.

So we have a two phase study, the micro transit one that is independent, some core public mass transit, and one that is bringing people in connecting to the core public mass transit. So we're looking at both of those probably within the next year. We'll have some pilots out to look at the effectiveness of it and start launching those around the region.

Paul Comfort: That's good. Yeah. I've already written a chapter that I'm going to use in the book on that topic of how micro transit can be used to improve equity and inclusion.

Because if you have to move 40 foot bus routes because there's not enough riders on them, you're still going to leave some people disenfranchised if you don't provide a layer of microtransit to help those who are still there.

So what's your vision for what it will look like if you did get where you want it to be for equity and inclusion? Have you like painted a picture in your mind of what it would be?

Julie Timm: I do have, I have two pictures in my mind. One picture in my mind is rainbows and unicorns. Well, they're linked arm and arm. And, you know, where we have the caring child and neighbor coming by picking Mary up and getting her somewhere and all of us taking responsibility, brotherhood and all that.

That's what drives me. I know that that is human nature. I had this dichotomy in my head. Rainbows and unicorns in reality. And my reality is pretty dark reality. If I can move the benchmark a little bit towards it, this idea where people don't think of themselves as "I'm not a bus person". What does that mean? So, you know, we're all bus people.

But that people aren't afraid to put their children on buses because they have this idea that the buses are filled with homeless folks and they they're afraid to be near them. And they're there, they're thinking it's the "gangster" and they're thinking it's the "criminal" and they're thinking it's the homeless person.

Moving the benchmark where people realize that the majority of transit riders aren't that and those are transit riders. Stop defining that portion of our population, our vulnerable populations as transit riders and redefine them as vulnerable and getting them health and services.

Paul Comfort: What would you say are some good first steps for a transit system who hasn't really done much in trying to improve their equity and inclusion to put on these new lenses and say, let's look at it here?

Julie Timm: I would say get on the bus. That's good. The first step is get on the bus and ride as much as you can and talk to your operators and talk to the people on the bus and get an origin destination survey that actually helps define who your demographics are by mode. So you understand who is riding and where they are going. That's a good place to start.

CHAPTER 7

INEZ EVANS

President & Chief Executive Officer
IndyGo

In conversation with Inez..

Paul Comfort: I'm with Inez Evans, CEO and President of IndyGo. Please tell me a little about yourself and your agency.

Inez Evans: The Indianapolis Public Transportation Corporation, or IndyGo, runs 30 routes, including one bus rapid transit line, known as the Red Line. We're getting ready to break ground this spring on the second of three BRT lines. It's called the Purple Line. The third line, the Blue Line, is in the design phase. These lines will be made up of an all-electric fleet, one of the largest BRT electric infrastructures in the country. We also run paratransit services for our riders with significant disabilities. We do not run rail.

A few other exciting projects we're working on include expanding our service in response to the 2016 referendum, which looks to increase services in our region at about 70%. Additionally, we've bought new facilities, including a campus for our headquarters. We desperately needed to expand our vehicle storage space, especially since we have 30+ BYD, 60-foot articulated buses. We're also looking at a whole host of other things, like potentially hydrogen fuel cells. We've recently launched a Coach Operator Apprenticeship Program and a full Workforce Development Program.

Paul Comfort: That's great. Tell me about your community and the area you serve. Is it just the City of Indianapolis or is it also some of the surrounding area?

Inez Evans: Great question. We serve all of Marion County. Indy is unique because we are bigger than Chicago when you look at square miles. Indianapolis is just about 400 square miles and that is a lot of area for our transit agency to cover. One of the things the referendum allows us to do is have dedicated funding for transit so we can address this issue, look at analyzing our service and make changes to expand our service so we can better service the entire county.

What we've discovered is maybe the 40-foot bus isn't the best vehicle to accomplish that everywhere. By using smaller buses, we can get more bang for our buck because the cost per hour to run those services is much less than the 40-foot bus.

Paul Comfort: Tell me about your workforce. How many employees do you have?

Inez Evans: We presently have about 772 employees. We should be sitting at 800, but just like every other transit agency across the nation, we are experiencing a shortage unlike anything we've ever seen. The pandemic has taken its toll on our workforce. Our professional coach operators work on the front lines with the public in confined spaces, which created some angst during the early part of the pandemic when there was so much uncertainty. However, we have gone the extra mile to ensure operator safety and protection against COVID-19, including providing them with masks. We also put up protective shields to create a protective barrier between operators and the riders. We also provide a deep cleaning on each bus daily to disinfect them. Additionally, free COVID-19 testing is available to all IndyGo employees, and we've partnered with the Marion County Public Health Department to provide the vaccines and booster shots at our downtown transit center three days a week. No appointment is necessary, and that clinic is open to the general public.

On top of the extensive measures to protect against the pandemic, we've also increased the starting pay for operators, and all employees have access to a number of perks, including a free health clinic onsite for employees and their families, free bus transportation for all employees and their families, excellent health benefits and much more. We are one of the best employers in the city and the state of Indiana and continue our robust recruiting efforts that are starting to pay off. Once we complete the Purple and Blue lines, we should be sitting at about 1,200 employees.

Paul Comfort: Wow. Are you going to outsource that operation or run it in-house?

Inez Evans: We look to continue to partner with our ATU Local 1070 union on our local services here in Indianapolis.

We're going to look at every way we can to be fiscally responsible for the agency, but we are confident that we'll be able to work through something with our ATU partners to be able to continue other services that will benefit our union members.

That doesn't mean that we haven't contracted portions of our services. We contract out our paratransit. But we've also looked at a lot of in-house janitorial services. They're called general laborers at IndyGo. We were able to contract those jobs out as a second chance employer at our Julia M. Carson Transit Center.

We changed our policy and created a second chance policy, which again, was looking at equity in our city. Our city was really promoting a second chance program because there are a significant number of individuals who qualify.

Paul Comfort: Is this for people that have been incarcerated?

Inez Evans: So, we looked at that, because the city partnered with a company in-house to bring individuals on board. We looked at the policies. I saw there were some things we could do, and we've had about five individuals successfully go through the program.

Our applications right now don't require applicants to immediately disclose anything about a criminal background and if something pops up, it remains private.

Our human resources department brings the employee in to have a private conversation with them about the circumstances surrounding the criminal offense.

There are some crimes that are not allowed. No crimes against children are allowed. We are a safe place organization. So, we can't have any crimes against children, or violent crimes against other individuals, such as rape. But we're very excited about it and hope to partner a little bit more with another organization to be able to become more of an employment center for when folks are immediately coming out of incarceration.

We want to get into the system and then have them filter directly into us. That's one of our programs that we're really excited about.

Paul Comfort: Great. In Baltimore we did something similar. We did it with a group that was training folks that were coming out of jail in mechanics, auto mechanics.

And they would actually start working with them while they're incarcerated. And then they were in this program and then we could hire them. The goal was that we would eventually hire them at the MTA to be bus mechanics. And I thought it was a great way. I mean, because not only are we short on drivers, you know, we also need skilled mechanics.

Inez Evans: Absolutely! Going into how technology has progressed, from starting as a diesel bus going into, CNG, LNG, and now electric, you need skilled workers. One of our apprenticeship programs will be taking individuals from a diesel technician to an electronic technician.

Along those lines, we are looking at ways we can go into high schools, as well as into the system, to see how we can partner with individuals to bridge that gap so they have gainful employment as soon as they graduate.

Paul Comfort: That's great. Tell me about your community and your workforce.

Inez Evans: Of our riders, 76% are employed. 71% of all riders are from households that earn less than $35,000. About 67% of our riders are persons of color. Our workforce closely mirrors our community. Of our nearly 800 employees, 75% are people of color.

Paul Comfort: Tell us some about the importance of programs with equity and inclusion at IndyGo and what you all are doing right now.

Inez Evans: I think transit systems should be built around equity, and IndyGo is no exception. We're here to serve the underserved. That's a lot of what we're doing with the Marion County Transit Plan. We've done a new comprehensive operational analysis, to focus on how we can execute it.

Given the projected dollars that are going to be available to us again, I've also brought in a new vice president of workforce development, diversity and inclusion to be part of our team. She has, in turn, created a brand new team that includes a manager of diversity and inclusion who works with individuals within the city.

Outside of the agency, I belong to the Greater Indianapolis Progress Committee (GIPC). GIPC was created to provide the mayor with a forum for considering, discussing and then providing recommendations on difficult issues facing the city.

I'm also on the arts council. So many of the things that we've worked on include making sure the individuals who we are doing business with the city are representing the demographics and the culture of the city. Too often, we focus on whether they have a DBE requirement. But, another important consideration is what does their organization look like?

We recently moved money from one bank to another because the diversity of the first bank wasn't representative of our community. We shared with them that there was nothing but older, Caucasian men who were sitting on their board and the leadership tier of their organization. I kept checking back and asking, "Hey guys, what are you doing to address the lack of equity and inclusion in your organization?"

I think what you're seeing is that a lot of transit agencies are starting to ask the question beyond just having a DBE program. We truly want to see how it's embedding itself into a diversity, equity and inclusion program. That is calling many businesses into question about how are they are truly representing the community.

Going back to the Marion County Transit Plan, like many other transit agencies, we're looking to see if fixed route service is really the best solution, especially in communities that are struggling and are blighted. Our numbers are showing that we're only getting about five passengers per hour in some neighborhoods. Typically, that should be a means for us to stop serving those areas. But, if we stop, they lose the one bridge they have and that's not good. So, we're working within our agency and within the city to come up with on-demand mobility as a service.

We're also looking at the sidewalks. How are people able to get to the transit stops? Our city needs about $7 billion in sidewalks. Sidewalks are all about accessibility. We're no different than anybody else. But, that's still an astronomical lift.

That's a challenge going forward that has stopped us from being able to expand in some areas. Because as you know, if you expand, you've got to have a stop that's accessible. But, it can't be just the 5x8 cement pad. You've got to make sure there's connectivity from point to point.

As you can guess, nobody has $7 billion sitting around to put in all the sidewalks needed at once. So we think of mobility as a service to bridge that gap to connect individuals.

Paul Comfort: I agree with that. I've actually written a chapter for this book and it's the only chapter I've written, about exactly that. On how micro transit is a key to do exactly what you said. If routes had to be moved because of ridership patterns, you don't want to leave anybody kind of disenfranchised. Right?

Inez Evans: Exactly! To add to that, what I think a lot of people are not talking about, is equity for persons with disabilities. You and I come from a background where we cut our teeth on paratransit.

I'm a mother of a disabled adult so I'm always focused on that lens. We're trying to work towards a program that is same day without the additional cost to the person. The ADA talks about accessibility and that we need to mirror the fixed route bus line and other things.

But do we really? Yes, we match area. We match time of the day. We can't go more than double the fare, but we don't match convenience. It's not the same as any one of us looking at our phones to see a bus will be there in 10 minutes that I can get on to reach my destination.

For same-day service, a paratransit rider must have a crystal ball that anticipates when they are going to run out of milk and need to go to the store or wake up sick and need to go to the doctor. But, then they get charged double the price if they can get a ride to go to the store or the doctor.

So, we are trying to fix that.

Paul Comfort: That's awesome. Yeah, I think just like what you said, they often are still marginalized in many ways, by the inconvenience of the service. And they're the ones who may need it the most because they can't drive.

And so, I think that's wonderful. Are you, in-house, are you looking at promotional practices and all that? Do you have committees, or any other kind of internal agency activitles going on when it comes to promoting equity?

Inez Evans: Absolutely! Our DBE department has grown. It used to be a department of one. We brought in consultants to help, especially with the Purple Line, doing these big, large contracts to make sure our contractors, or those who are sub-contracting with these individuals, are paying their folks appropriately and that their hiring practices are including the lens of our community.

They meet on a regular basis to make sure everyone is doing what they're supposed to do. We have held many classes in the last year to help individuals understand that and what it means to become a DBE, WBE or anything with the "E's" on it.

Then, we took it a step further and started to hold webinars. That's when we noticed the proposals were written poorly. So, we piloted a writing program to help individuals understand how to respond to proposals. I think a lot of times we, as transit agencies, simply hand people a DBE form and tell them to fill it out.

So, we are trying to do better. We surveyed many people. We have these meetings, and all these people will show up and say, "Yay, we're going to bid on your project." And then we only get a small number. That made us start asking why we were not getting more people to bid on our projects.

The feedback we got is that the vendors were overwhelmed. They told us it was too much. So, we started to break down the programs into smaller nuggets, and we're finding people are experiencing more success. That doesn't just benefit us. As part of IndyGo, you are also certified with the state and with the city.

We have a DBE goal, and then we have the other goals as two separate goals for our organization. We have committees that include our drivers, mechanics and administrative employees, which are all a part of the culture engagement team.

And then they have a diverse diversity, equity and inclusion committee as well. They put together initiatives and bring them to the executive team. From there, we discuss what our deficiency is and what we need to do to improve it.

Paul Comfort: That's great. And it sounds like you have a really good relationship with your unions. Are they involved at all in these efforts?

Inez Evans: Absolutely. It is so important to have the union leadership at the table when having these conversations, because again, they represent 80% of the workforce here at the agency. You need to have that buy-in within the communities. You know, within any strategic plan, it is a bottom-up and top-down thing. I want to say it's more of a circle instead because we're all equal when it comes to sitting at the table and doing the work.

Paul Comfort: That's great. Anything else you want to share about efforts you're making in the area of equity and inclusion that I haven't asked you specifically about?

Inez Evans: We talked about changing the service. I mean, we're looking at different technologies to bridge the gap. You know, not everyone has a smartphone, so we were able to get a grant through the FTA to work on a mobility concierge program. You can actually call the phone number to our call center, which we changed from having a fixed route call center and a paratransit call center into one center.

This way, we're able to bridge the gap between people with disabilities and our non-paratransit riders. We can also provide the best service possible, so that when the concierge program takes off for the microtransit individuals who don't have a smartphone to use, they can just call the number, and a person at the desk will take care of getting that ride scheduled for them.

Paul Comfort: Oh, that's great. Is that something you've already done?

Inez Evans: We've pulled the centers together. We haven't launched the mobility concierge because we're waiting to start our first microtransit. It would have already started, but unfortunately, because of this thing called COVID, we couldn't get the buses in order to pull the microtransit off.

As soon as we can get the buses, we are ready.

Paul Comfort: That's great. I haven't heard of any other agencies doing that. So is this a place where ADA clients would call in to make a reservation and now you've combined that with your customer service center?

Inez Evans: We looked at it from a standpoint that there are peak times for paratransit. We are always struggling when paratransit service ends at 6 p.m. and everyone is rushing at 5:45 p.m., trying to get through to the call center. It's hard to schedule for that. When you've got fixed route call center agents that might not be as busy at that time why not combine forces to provide more people answering phones to help? If you have a paratransit person who is eligible from a trip-by-trip perspective to ride fixed route, why not have that discussion more in real-time and not have to transfer them and all that stuff?

We are really focusing a lot more on the customer experience.

I think folks have been focusing on ridership, ridership, ridership, and I think we need to start talking about the rider's experience. We should be less focused on how many people are in the seats and more focused on ensuring those who are riding with us are getting the best service possible.

So whether you're on the bus, a bicycle, rideshare, taxi, or trying to traverse on the sidewalk. We should be a part of that.

Paul Comfort: That's great. We really touched some areas in the interview that I haven't discussed with anybody else. Thank you.

CHAPTER 8

BRAD MILLER

Chief Executive Officer
Pinellas Suncoast Transit Authority

Let's Hear From Brad....

Paul Comfort: So, Brad, tell me about your system.

Brad Miller: Okay. Well, we are down here in beautiful St. Petersburg, which is on the west coast of Florida. It's in the larger Tampa Bay region of the state. Our transit system's operations provide service to about half of the Tampa Bay Region's urban population, about a million people in the area our buses serve.

And for tourists and beach lovers, we are the best half of the Tampa Bay area because our area includes the Gulf beaches. This means we have a big tourist-oriented economy in the area that my agency serves. We have about 900 employees, about 250 buses and trolley buses, plus an innovative contracted paratransit system. We are always working hard to serve the employees' needs in this tourist-based economy and, of course, lots of people that are not from here come down here to the best beaches in the world.

Clearwater Beach, St. Pete Beach, all of our beaches are just awesome. Our highest ridership period of the year is always during Spring Break. We're one of the only transit systems I know of with a "wet bathing suit policy" because our trolleys go up and down Gulf Boulevard very close to the sand. It's not as much of a commuter market like other transit systems serve and like other systems I've worked for, but it's still a pretty great place to be.

We don't really have a lot of people wearing business suits and ties on a daily basis in our market and we don't really have a large downtown business core. We have a service economy in all parts of our service area, including hotel and restaurant jobs. Many tourists visit here without their cars. So, they take advantage of our transit system.

Paul Comfort: You've been very innovative, Brad. I remember visiting you a few years ago at the Florida Transit Association meeting and you were one of the first ones to get Uber or Lyft as part of your mobility system. You've been very innovative. Tell us about some of the innovations you brought in.

Brad Miller: I'm very honored to lead an organization that has received recognition for being able to think outside the box. I'm always looking to the future, to innovative options that will make our transportation system in our community better. And, we've had a lot of great success with partnerships with TNCs like Uber and Lyft. We started off as the very first transit system in the country to have a contract with Uber about six or seven years ago when we launched a successful first mile, last mile program.

What is our most recent innovation? Over the last couple of years, we have completely transformed our paratransit program into a real mobility on demand program where we have Uber and Lyft, taxis, and different wheelchair companies that are our contractors.

We basically provide the best trip for a person with a disability. If they can go in a car and they want to go right now they get an Uber. If they have a doctor's appointment tomorrow and they need a wheelchair then they can get a van.

It's been really exciting to see that transformation and to see how the passengers love it. They love being able to not just go to doctor's appointments but also go to Applebee's to see their daughter for lunch on a whim. It's been a really, great program. We are really proud of the innovations we've implemented, and we think they're making transit better here in St. Petersburg.

Paul Comfort: Is that service still just for ADA?

Brad Miller: Well, we also have a number of other partnerships that are for anybody. All riders can get an Uber or Lyft or taxi ride to and from a bus stop if they don't live near one. That's open to anybody. Additionally, we have a late-night program that's designed for lower income riders, who finish work late at night after the buses stop running, and they can get a discounted Uber ride home.

Paul Comfort: APTA told me that your agency was the first one to sign their new commitment to equity and inclusion. Tell us about that.

Brad Miller: Prior to getting involved with APTA's equity initiative, which I'm really very grateful for how APTA has stepped up in such a big way taking the lead for the whole industry, PSTA had already started to look internally at our organization.

I'm sure most transit systems were just like PSTA, starting in the middle of 2020, examining how we can be more forward facing, proactive in showing that we are a diverse, equitable, and inclusive organization from a number of different perspectives. One primary perspective of course is our own workforce.

I strongly believe making sure that we have a diverse workforce makes our transportation services work better. We took a hard look at the hiring and interviewing process at PSTA from the beginning; from where we recruit, to how we bring people in the door for different jobs, to how that process all works; all the processes involved with deciding who we hire.

Then, once new employees get here, we examined who we promote and who gets workforce development opportunities. It's a whole process.

Additional to examining the hiring and promoting processes, PSTA looked at the way our transit services have been designed over the years. That's a longer process that's ongoing.

Some routes, like all the systems I've worked at, have not changed since 1902 or they were a streetcar route back in the day. Maybe back then they weren't put in the spot where they needed to be or maybe they were put there for other, non-equitable reasons.

As part of this equitable service analysis, we are also taking a holistic look at all our transit centers and shelters. That's still going on.

Finally the third emphasis PSTA made for equity was this idea of being inclusive in our community. We had a voting campaign to make sure all our employees were registered to vote and then went and voted.

We did raffles. If you showed your voting sticker, then you could get a gift card. We had a competition to see which group within the agency could get the most people to vote. It was really fun.

Those three efforts, hiring, service analysis, and community engagement were just the start at PSTA. Most recently, we started formally creating "employee resource groups." Different groups within the organization created by employees. They're open to any employee and are designed to highlight certain types of employees such as a Multicultural group, which highlights folks who come from different countries or have family members from different countries. That's been really successful. We also started a LGBTQ group, a People with Disabilities group, a Veterans group, and a Working Mothers group.

Paul Comfort: That's great. Is it okay if I dig in some of these groups? Maybe you give me a little more detail.

Brad Miller: Absolutely

Paul Comfort: Okay. So, on the employee resource groups, how does your agency support them?

Brad Miller: Right now, we have a small amount of funding set aside to support them.

It's really up to each individual group what they want to do. I think the Multicultural group will sponsor some food events and lunches and even some fun outings to different restaurants in the area. Right now, we're in the midst of planning to get the word out to the whole organization to have a type of fair or open house where they're all represented. That's how the agency supports these employee groups.

Paul Comfort: Are they involved in making recommendations for your agency at all?

Brad Miller: Yes. For example, the group that is focusing on issues around people with disabilities are specifically making recommendations on ways in which we want to make our system, our facilities, and our office building more accessible to more people.

Paul Comfort: That's good. On the routes themselves, you said you're doing an analysis of the routes to make sure that they're more equitable and inclusive. Can you tell me any more about that? What are you looking for or where are you on that?

Brad Miller: We regularly look at all our routes and services, but like I said, our service is based on a tourism-based economy. We know that one of our highest ridership routes is along Gulf Boulevard, right along the beach by all those hotels.

Our services are somewhat fixed in place with very little adjustments in the last few decades, but we've tried to peel it back a little bit just in the last say two years to look to our past and the decisions that were made and why they were made.

Our largest community, the city of St. Petersburg, has just come out with a race and equity plan or study of how the city evolved with a number of recommendations. We're in partnership with that effort looking at whether our bus shelters are placed in an equitable manner.

Even the ones that have been there forever or in areas that that are missing one or don't have the transit amenities; making sure that all of it is done in an equitable manner as well.

Paul Comfort: Great. And now onto your employees, you've mentioned that you've maybe changed up your recruiting, hiring, and promotional practices. Can you give us any details on any of the changes you made so that other transit agencies might be able to look at this as an example?

Brad Miller: Of course, first I think every transit system can start with a baseline of what we turn into the federal government with data from EEO reports, which we turn in on a quarterly basis. Then we at PSTA took a look at what other information is out there that explains who you/we have sitting in our office chairs or in your bus operator's seat. I think it's important for transit systems to take a critical look at their own practices.

We looked at the processes that our HR department uses and the way we recruit because you can only hire people that you interview, and you can only interview people that apply for the jobs. We dramatically expanded our reach for advertising our jobs, beyond the typical websites like indeed.com and monster.com.

So, starting from that basic ground level and then started collecting the data – to the extent that people are willing to share – on who's applying. From there, we're tracking the next step of who we are choosing for interviews just to see how that looks. And from there, we now track who we offer jobs to and who takes the job along the way. It's really interesting just the mere fact that we are tracking all this now and that people are feeling it has raised awareness.

Paul Comfort: The hiring process itself, have you changed anything? I know we at MTA in Baltimore, we had a rule that there had to be three people on an interview committee and they had to be gender and racial diversity on the interview committees. Have you all done anything like that?

Brad Miller: We have for certain jobs yes but we also want experts on the subject we're hiring for to participate in the panels, it just depends on the job. For some jobs, it's very technical and to have somebody that doesn't really know anything about it, it doesn't make much sense.

Another idea we talked about, which was just a random brainstorm I had, well, not a brainstorm, but as a sports fan I thought, why don't we do the Rooney rule. Why can't we do what the NFL does, where one of the people that you interview for every job must be a minority.

After a lot of debate within my agency, and after my lawyers questioned whether I was allowed to do the Rooney rule we decided against implementing it formally, but we talked about it a lot. Maybe it's not a hard and fast rule we have necessarily for every job, but I think the fact that we talked about it, has raised awareness and produced more candidates and more minority candidates. So that's been key.

Paul Comfort: Finally, on your promotional practices, what you mentioned that you had taken a look at that, what have you done differently there?

Brad Miller: We're tracking who is being offered, volunteering, or taking advantage of workforce development opportunities and how that breaks down as far as our own internal programs like candidates for Leadership APTA, APTA's Emerging Leaders Program, or other state training programs. And we're just starting to look at promotions and the way those are handled. Who are the candidates for a promotion and are there more than one person being considered? Those kinds of questions are all reflective of our stated commitment to diversity, equity, and inclusion.

Paul Comfort: That's great. Anything else that you want to mention before we wrap up the interview on what you're doing in this.

Brad Miller: Two things. 1) we do have an official DEI council within the organization. This is made up of employees from all the different departments. They are the brains behind everything I've just talked to you about. They have come up with these ideas and pushed them forward and really organized everything. They're a really active group themselves so, that's very exciting to me.

Finally, while this commitment is something I very strongly believe in as one of my own core values towards helping others, I also think this commitment to diversity and equity also benefits me and my agency. I know for our agency and myself to have success, I must get really good candidates to apply for our jobs and we have to hire superior talented individuals. So, the way I get the best candidates coming to work for me is if they go on our website and see there are people like them working here, they see we have a welcoming culture here at PSTA. I am putting pictures of these groups on our website and highlighting them so that outside candidates can see themselves working here. They might say, "maybe I don't really know the white guy that's in the CEO job is all about but I can find a home at PSTA, I feel comfortable applying for a job there.

Paul Comfort: That's great. Thanks Brad. Those are great efforts you're making there.

CHAPTER 9

PAUL TOLIVER

APTA Hall of Fame & "CEO Whisperer"

Paul's History of Equity & Inclusion in public transportation

Paul Comfort: Paul, tell us about your background and experience in the public transit industry.

Paul Toliver: Okay. I have been around for a few years. I started in 1973.

I came in fresh from graduate school and deliberately sought out a position in the public transit industry. I started out looking at the total transportation field and even applied for positions with airlines, railroads (freight and passenger) and ultimately I focused on public transit. Some of my friends accused me of being a kid that would go over to the streetcar barn and pull the streetcar poles off the wires. Of course I denied it, but somehow transit got into my blood. I was young and just finished graduate school when I deliberately sought out a position in transit and specifically in Cincinnati.

The transit system was transitioning from a private company called Cincinnati Transit Incorporated to a public system like most cities were going through at this time in history. I just paid attention to what the newspapers were saying about how the system was going to be managed. The papers reported that the Southwest Ohio Regional Transit Authority (SORTA) was this new agency named to run the system. I then, just walked in to the offices of SORTA and met the Executive Director and talk to him about, you know, working with the transit system.

He mentioned that they were going to hire a management firm to run the company as opposed to hiring their own staff. They would take over the existing staff of the private company. The owners and/or the senior executives of the private company would be the only ones leaving. So, what I did was to continue to pay attention to who was leading the charge to be named to manage the system.

That led me to a firm called ATE Management, Inc. (ATE). ATE was headquartered in Cincinnati, Ohio. It looked like this local company would get the nod to manage that company. They in fact did get the contract to manage the day to day operations of this new entity called SORTA. ATE was a spinoff of American Transportation Enterprises, which was a private company that owned bus companies around country. ATE was ultimately purchased by Ryder, Inc. and then "First Group" of England purchased ATE from Ryder.

The transit system was given the "public nickname" of Queen City Metro. This was my beginning in 1973. ATE actually started managing the operations of the system in the summer of 1973 and I was one of the first three (3) individuals named as the senior executive team to run the system under contract to the Transit Authority.

We were not employees of the transit authority, we were under contract. It is not like we see today with contract management firms that provide all the employees. ATE also provided support services such as labor negotiations, transit planning, route and schedule development, and procurement and marketing. I started off as Director of Operations Planning and Research. The positions of Director of Operations Planning, Research and even Transit Marketing were new positions that the private systems did not have.

This was the era when the transit industry is being introduced to these individuals coming out of college as opposed to up through the ranks. It was an interesting way to begin. To get indoctrinated to transit operations, we newbies got thrown into the nitty gritty world of the Comprehensive Operational Analysis (COA). In the early days, prior to automatic passenger counters, computers, tablets and wireless communications, we followed buses in cars from the first morning pull-out to the last pull-in that night. We drove cars behind the bus and wrote down information on long strips of paper with printed bus stop names and recorded the number of passengers boarding and deboarding at that stop, we recorded time between stops, made observations about the route, traffic, where were passengers going after they deboarded and other relevant data.

I did this type of work for the first three months before we took over the Cincinnati operations when I was assigned to the management ranks at Queen City Metro. This is how in started in 1973. It was new, we were making the rules as we went along but more than anything, it was fun.

Paul Comfort: And where'd you go then?

Paul Toliver: Well, you've heard me talk about having to move.

At Queen City Metro, I was in planning. We did a lot of great things in Cincinnati. I, however, wanted to move up and there were a lot of people ahead of me. As transit operators say, when someone leaves, "what was his seniority number"? An opportunity did come when ATE asked me if I'd like to take the Assistant General Manager for Operations position three and a half years later in Tulsa, OK. I took that position for eighteen months. I then got an opportunity to become the CEO of my own transit system in South Bend, Indiana. The home of the current US Secretary of Transportation. I accepted that position in 1978. South Bend was my first taste of being a CEO. I was also the fourth African American transit system CEO in the industry,

Other African American CEOs soon followed. This was in the late seventies, and it was new territory for all of us. One more time, it was our version of the "wild west" where rules were now being written for managing a **public transit system** as opposed to running a "bus company"! We were all new faces and we were now having to deal with all the issues of being the first. I have to give credit to ATE, which was a private company, to its young Harvard educated Executive Vice President,

Phil Ringo, who bit the bullet and began hiring people of color and women to fill senior management positions for the transit system's managed by ATE.

This young Executive VP realized that ATE's clients are going to be in major urban communities. And he figured that if he's going to push a product, "**people**", he had better have some people who look like me if he was going be successful. Some of ATE's major clients included Baltimore, Richmond, Norfolk, Cincinnati, Louisville, Memphis, Nashville, Kansas City and New Orleans.

That gave ATE M&S a leg up when it came to competing for management contracts in these major urban community. He was smart, very smart. He's still out here somewhere. He moved into other industries and made his fortune, but I want to give a lot of credit to somebody who figured it out early in the game.

I was one of those folks he brought in early in the game. I was the second black professional after a man named John Potts who is still on the scene. I, then, recruited people like Will Scott and Bobby Griffin. John Potts recruited Maxine Marshall and Al Richards. Frank Martin and Ron Barnes were recruited by Will Scott. We all came in this way. And it is still today a lesson on how to increase and deal with diversity and inclusion. A lot of us are now retiring, being there in the beginning of the transition of this industry from private to public as well as being a part of "**writing the rules" allowed us to not only survive but thrive.**

MY CALLING

I soon realized my preference was not a small city. South Bend was great but it was a small city and a small system. We ran 35 buses all day long with 30 minute headways all day, it didn't change in the off peak. It was operated six days a with no Sunday service and every bus was off the street by 7:00 PM.

Those parameters don't really work today even in South Bend. However, I knew I wanted to go into a bigger market, bigger system and a bigger challenge. I got the opportunity to go to work (as part of ATE) for the Mayor of New Orleans as an advisor to the Mayor's Office of Transit Administration (OTA).

In 1981, moved to New Orleans to become the "Advisor to the Mayor's Office of Transit Administration (OTA). The transit system was still being operated by a private company, New Orleans Public Service Incorporated (NOPSI). The job of the advisor was to review and confirm the amount and accuracy of the subsidy the City of New Orleans was paying to NOPSI to support the bus service operated for the citizens of New Orleans. The amount the city subsidized the private company in the early 80's was approximately $8 million per year.

This confirmation was based on eligible expenses with which this private company said they needed help. As an accountant by education, it was a natural role to verify expense numbers as well as to verify the subsidy number.

The City of New Orleans moved to purchase the assets of the transit system from a willing NOPSI. Fred Gilliam and I were the two chief negotiators on behalf of the city to purchase NOPSI's assets. The rest of the team was comprised of attorneys, actuaries, appraisers and accountants.

The New Orleans Regional Transit Authority which had been created by the State of Louisiana a year earlier was in line to operate those assets as the new "New Orleans Regional Transit System (RTA)".

Operations of this new RTA began in 1983. I moved into the role of Assistant General Manager of Operations. Fred Gillam moved into the role of General Manager. The Executive Director of the Authority as well as the individual that hired ATE to manage the day-to-day operations was named Dean Bell, who himself was quite a legend and visionary.

Dean left New Orleans in the nineties and joined Montgomery Watson as a water industry consultant but give him credit for bringing ATE in to help make this transition successful.

New Orleans, as many remember, ran into some tough times, economically, when the oil and gas industry went belly up in the mid-eighties. I knew that that it was time to seek greener pastures. There was also a new Mayor elected and as most appointed officials know, the newly elected usually will want their own person. I had always wanted to go to the west coast, so I strategized how to make my way west. Ultimately, through networking and relationships, Dutch Morial, (then Mayor of New Orleans) had a fraternity brother who was head of the public services commission in San Francisco.

He introduced me and 18 months later, I applied to the City of San Francisco for the position of Deputy General Manager/Chief Transportation Officer for the San Francisco Municipal Railway (aka Muni). I was subsequently named to fill that position. I moved to San Francisco in 1984 and began working in the Mayor Diane Feinstein Administration as the Deputy General Manager/Chief Transportation Officer for the San Francisco Municipal Railway. You may remember, she was sworn in as Mayor after the assassination of Mayor George Moscone and Councilmember Harvey Milk in 1978. She is still very active as the Senior Senator from the State of California.

Muni operated and still does operate a major light rail operation (the 2nd largest light rail system in the country) as well as streetcars, cable cars, trolley buses and diesel buses. Muni is a true multimodal agency with a grand mix of all sorts of equipment operating on the *streets of San Francisco*. It was, for me, a great system of which to be a part.

In 1988, I got a call from a headhunter that said Seattle was seeking a Director for their transit system. I informed him that I wanted to stay on the west coast. I was not that well-traveled quite yet (smile). He said to me, "Seattle is the west coast you dummy!"

I went to Seattle for the interview and fell in love with the city. Accepting this position was best move that I have made both professionally and personally in my career and life for they had money, a culture of excellence and it was a beautiful place to live.

The initial position for which I was hired was for the Director for the 1,200 all bus transit system which was part of the Metropolitan Municipality of Seattle commonly referred to as Seattle Metro. It was a separate and independent State created agency to provide Public Transit and Waste Water Treatment to the citizens of King County (WA) as well as parts of three other counties. Seattle Metro accomplished many great things including building this country's only underground subway for buses which is 3½ miles roadway underneath Seattle's downtown core. It is now used for the underground tunnel for the Sound Transit light rail operation.

In 1996, Seattle Metro was merged into King County government. Seattle Metro was an entity with a different culture, with different values and whose motto was

"Better Than Promised". Basically, it was a takeover by a government with a different culture and different values. I think it was the biggest mistake in history of public policy in the state of Washington. This merger happened because a court said this agency which has existed for 25 years is unconstitutional under the constitution of the State of Washington.

It was a masterful move by a county "political machine" to provide a reason for these same county politicians have a reason to exist as a viable county government in the face of numerous newly created cities and annexations.

This author felt that there were other ways to solve the constitutional problem such as creating a separate Transit Authority like other regions around the country. I guess you can see that I'm not a fan of city governments or county governments operating a public transit system.

In 1996, Seattle Metro transitioned into county government and I was named to head the newly created King County Department of Transportation. I stayed for six more years, as its Director. The department included roads & bridges in unincorporated King County, a major world class transit system called King County Metro, a local airport (Boeing Field), and a major county vehicle maintenance shop for all types of vehicles. As the Director of the County's Department of Transportation, I worked for and reported to two County Executives. The first was Gary Locke. Gary later became the Governor of the State of Washington and then served in the Obama Cabinet and as well as serving as Ambassador of China. The second County Executive was Ron Sims and he later served as Deputy Secretary of HUD.

After 6 years as Director, I went on my own and I've been on my own since 2002 except for when I left Seattle in 2013 to work in Detroit under a contract to be a part of the MV Transit, Inc who was contracted to help the city work through bankruptcy. I worked and lived in Detroit a little more the three years until the city emerged from bankruptcy and was then able to hire its own City employees to operate the transit system.

Paul Comfort: That's a fascinating career story, Paul. And you live in Florida now, right?

Paul Toliver: That is correct. Yeah, and I still get back to Seattle to try and escape the heat of the summer whenever I can.

Paul Comfort: So, tell some stories about historical inclusion and equity and what you think of the state of the industry now in public transit, helping to provide better equity inclusion in cities around the country.

Paul Toliver: I think there's a lot of push today on ensuring that there is equity in the services provided. In the beginning we focused on moving (some actually used the word hauling) people to the downtown urban center. The industry kept following that philosophy for a while after the industry transitioned to publicly operated agencies. This meant we made sure that there was a peak hour service which dropped off drastically during the mid-day and then picked back up during the afternoon peak.

In the late sixties, seventies and eighties ridership in most cities began to stop growing and even decline. We had become a nation of automobiles and everything else was considered second class transportation. In the late eighties, the industry began to take steps to try and reverse this trend by touting the environmental benefits of public transit as well as cost savings as compared to the auto. Running concurrently with the environmental movement was a ***re-awakening*** in the movement for civil and human rights for those whom our society had forgotten, ignored and dismissed over the last decade. A new generation of educated post-Vietnam political leaders were taking charge in major urban cities. They were listening to some very loud voices from women and minority groups who were demanding a change in how business in society was being carry out. The new political leaders in these major urban areas like Atlanta, Chicago, Cleveland, Baltimore, Cincinnati, Kansas City Houston, Los Angeles and Oakland were leading the charge for more equity in how resources were be allocated for services provided by the public sector.

The Federal Government was first targeted which resulted in more investments in housing, health care and public transportation. These new resources came with new requirements for more diversity and even more equity in how these resources were to be allocated. However, this focus on diversity and equity only applied to the federally funded projects while most local government still catered to the wealthier communities from where they perceived the source of their largest public contributions (aka tax revenues).

This new 21st Century re-awakening around diversity and equity is following two serious recessions and two decades of a leadership on both federal and local levels that understands that the only way for our total society to become fairer, old systems, old ways and old harmful thinking needs to change if all citizens are going to be treated fairly. So now we are seeing new faces, more ethnicities, new genders sitting in decision making chairs that can make a difference. These new decision makers are reprioritizing their customers based on how to benefit the total community as opposed to a few. The new decision makers, however, do have new technologies that are helping them solve some of the issues which were a challenge to us transit operators in the 20th century.

For instance, many of the new mobility based last mile service solutions (i.e. ride-sharing, bicycle paths, flexible and autonomous system) are becoming win-win solutions for more customers whether you be a "have or have not". This issue of resource allocation to the "have and have not" communities was one of my issues in Seattle. The then solution was a negotiated political formula for how much each of the three major regions received as measured by the cost of transit service.

That formula solution describes how we had to distribute resources in terms of service. We ended up for a decade or more chasing this white collar employee who had numerous mobility option including public transit. Yes, we were very successful in capturing a higher-than-average share of white collar commuters on public transit, but at what cost to the total community, especially to those who proved that they truly needed and were deserving of the service.

Recently in this 21st century, our industry is starting to realize, if it's going to change for the better, the industry has to refocus on ensuring that all people in the community, especially those who have no other means of mobility than public transit, receive a more equitable share of the public resources.

I called it a fairer treatment based on need, as opposed to some other criteria. In the eighties, we were looking at different criterion such as development and policies that would enhance development. Those policies took resources from the urban community where we had a high degree of underserved citizens to those areas where we wanted more development.

MANY CITY DWELLERS WERE MOVING TO THE CHEAPER SUBURBS

To make transit even more of a challenge, many of transit traditional customers were now leaving the city for the suburbs. This migration was forcing us to ask how do we serve both markets, those who remain the urban dweller transit user and the new suburban transit user with *no additional tax revenues*. In our quest to serve our suburban customer, the service to urban communities was no longer a priority. I think our industry has come full circle in this 21st century and is now asking, how do we serve all citizens and keep as a priority those who do not have.

Over the two last years, I've been involved with New Orleans and Seattle, two communities that are restructuring their transit service to elevate equity as their top priority. They are increasing frequencies on new and more relevant routes with new modern and appropriately size vehicles for lifeline users while finding new ways to serve the less frequent user communities. Much of this shift to equity as a top priority is a result of new transit system leaders that are now in the C-suite of the industry who are more focused on equity. Leaders like Terry White of Seattle and Alex Wiggins of New Orleans are at the front of the pack.

We now have these new leaders on the scene who have this vision of equity and inclusion and they are now drilling these values down throughout their organizations. I believe, we lost these values during the late 20th century and the early two thousands when we began to focus on new techniques, technologies and developing new transit focused communities because we wanted desperately to deal with issues like environment, sprawl and energy conservation. Maybe we started to share our few precious resources too thin. We started providing carpools, vanpools and other new mobility technologies that provided services as a way of enticing those who could afford more and had many more options available.

As we were chasing that suburban dream and taking resources from those that needed them more, these new transit leaders began to realize that we needed to figure out how can we serve a broader and a very deserving community if we truly believe that equity is much as a priority as the priorities the environment and development.

CHAPTER 10

NATALIE (TILLY) LOUGHBOROUGH

General Manager
Metro Trains Melbourne

Tilly and her team tell me about....

Equity and Inclusion in Australia's Metro Trains Melbourne Operations

In looking into international efforts to bring more equity and inclusion to public transport agencies, I heard from Natalie (Tilly) Loughborough, General Manager - Passenger Experience for Metro Trains Melbourne (MTM), the suburban rail service for Melbourne, Australia. She wanted to share with me what they have doing in this area and some of their successes, both for the organisation and for the individuals involved.

When I asked Tilly about her perspectives on equity and inclusion in the workplace at MTM she asserted that for her there's "two angles from my perspective in the diversity space being responsible for passenger experience."

She said that clearly one of them is around the customer experience in creating an inclusive and integrated network, not just in the city of Melbourne but also working collaboratively across the state of Victoria to make sure that they have got good transit offerings regardless of which service people want to use.

She continued that the other side of that, and "where we've been doing a lot of work is around having a workforce that reflects the communities we serve."

Tilly stated there has been a lot of effort at her agency put into promoting females into senior leadership roles and into those "historically male dominated roles". But also, she continued there has been effort around those who wouldn't usually be able to access employment. So, she says, "a lot of our work last year in the recruitment space went into looking at how not only can we bring people into roles like train driving and some of our Authorised Officers (and we've done really, really well there) but also how can we make sure that we further reflect the community we serve with the people who come into those roles."

She points to work over the past year trying to bring people in who "otherwise wouldn't be able to access employment because of maybe their prior immigration status, or individuals who have escaped domestic violence and are seeking to get on the employment ladder".

She's proud of some of the success they've had in creating those employment opportunities and supporting people on that journey into the business. Most recently she says bringing that and the pandemic together they also worked with the Department of Jobs Precincts and Regions, and the Department of Transport, to bring in a group of people who would otherwise not have been employed due to the pandemic. The Department of Jobs, Precincts and Regions had a fund that invested in getting people back into the workplace whose employment was directly impacted by the pandemic and MTM utilised it for bringing that "along with the enhanced hygiene requirements together. To then bring people onto the network, both from our perspective and our supplier's perspective to give short term work where it might not otherwise have been available to give people that leg up to get back into the workplace."

These were jobs like project manager and presentation officers who were going out and looking at the network and their subcontractors and suppliers, cleaning staff and supervisor positions who were delivering on the front line and enhancements required during the peak of the pandemic to encourage people back to the train network. Now they are working on defining some of the type skill sets and the people they need to bring into the organization for those functions.

Tilly says they've had, for instance, one of the individuals who came into their Authorised Officer (AO) cohort who fled their country because of the volatile situation. Authorised Officers (AO) are part of a team that works to keep Metro passengers safe, educate on ticketing and assist in keeping the train network running smoothly.

One such employee is **Betelhem Zeleke**, an AO who came to Australia by herself as an asylum seeker from Ethiopia at age 20. MTM recently celebrated a World Refugee Day virtual event with guest speakers including Betelhem. More than 300 people turned into the event that was at capacity, with many leaving positive comments.

BETELHEM'S STORY

Following the bombing of her university graduation ceremony in Ethiopia, Betelhem fled her country and was brought to Australia. Arriving in Darwin, Betelhem was taken to Naru where she spent over two years. No one else spoke her language, so Betelhem learned to speak and understand five languages while in detention.

Betelhem was transferred to a Brisbane detention centre where she spent a further two years before moving into community detention. After a landmark decision in 2018 she was released to find people supporting the rights of her and the others that were on one of the last boats to arrive on Australia shores. Betelhem still had many challenges to face – not knowing anyone, where to live, how to navigate transport or ways to make ends meet. Her move to Melbourne was an opportunity for Betelhem to heal from her detention experiences and to start a new life.

Joining Metro as an Authorised Officer in 2019, Betelhem has found a new family with her AO crew. In her role, Betelhem brings resilience and a positive energy, and is always on the look out to help passengers who may be confused and lost – as she once was.

Betelhem has become an advocate, supporting the human rights of other refugees and asylum seekers.

In addition to Betelhem's story here is the story of **Husnia**, another one of MTM's Authorised Officers who has resettled in Melbourne.

HUSNIA'S STORY

In 2018 Husnia arrived in Australia with her sister Fatima and their family after fleeing Pakistan as Afghani Asylum Seekers. They were recognised and tar-geted in Pakistan, and eventually had the means to seek refuge in Australia. Now permanent residents, they feel grateful for the safety and opportunities they have in Australia.

After learning about the Metro values from her sister Fatima, who works as a trainee administration assistant, Husnia decided to attend an information session and apply for the role as an AO. She was one of eight successful candidates from a diverse background who started their training in October of 2019.

Husnia believes that the resilience she has built from her experiences coming from a war-torn country has shaped and strengthened her to manage the day-to-day safety critical components of her role as an AO.

Husnia and Fatima together had the following advice for Refugees in Australia looking for work: "Don't feel alone and left out. You are in an entire new world. Explore Australia. The more you ask questions and be social the better chance you have"

Tilly says there are other employees like Betelhem and Husnia that have come through all of these sorts of very tough situations and have managed to be supported into a job there within the Metro Trains Melbourne organisation. She says there's a couple of other examples of apprenticeship style roles where they brought people in, they've got that opportunity and then they're able to flourish in other roles in the business. She states, "It's that kind of first step and leg up into something that might not otherwise have been an opportunity that was created for them."

MTM has a very small but effective team of individuals in the diversity space who do work to support people into these roles. They've had some good successes with people who wouldn't usually get into employment, "such as those who may have autism, for instance, or learning difficulties of some description. We've managed to support quite a few people who didn't have the confidence due to dyslexia, for instance, into the business".

Tilly continues, "So all of those things that are life's rich tapestry and knowing more about them, we can support people better. Which means that we can work through that and create the opportunities in the right space because not every role is right for everybody. But in the right space we can get people that opportunity to then develop." She has some other fantastic stories about how people are flourishing in the customer service space because of having that opportunity.

One has come in through the "socially responsible employment route" and that route has brought her into a Leading Station Assistant role, a frontline customer service position in a rail station. Tilly says, "She has come into a part time role and gained confidence in the role. Her confidence was a little low on entering the role due to her dyslexia but is an absolute wealth of ideas of what can be done on the network and she's starting to gradually realise that in a supported environment, this does not need to hinder her progress. She's been supported by her Station leaders to come out with the ideas and get into the workplace and really start and bring it all to the to the job. She feels comfortable to show the type of things she can do which at the beginning of the journey she wouldn't have otherwise been able to do."

Tilly says there are others in the Authorised Officer space who have come through significant domestic violence scenarios. MTM provides training around how to handle conflict. Tilly asserts that training "doesn't just give them the skills in the workplace. It allows them to have better skills in handling those situations in their personal lives. So, it is hopefully helping that all-round picture at least a little rather than just the workplace piece."

ENGINEERING CADET PROGRAM

Another way to attract and retain a diverse workforce is to work with partner agencies to set up formal outreach programs. One such program is the Level Crossing Removal Project (LXRP). The program has unlocked exciting opportunities for asylum seekers and refugees to kick-start their engineering careers on some of Victoria's biggest transport projects as part of the Engineering Pathways Industry Cadetship – or EPIC – program.

The EPIC program, led by LXRP and supported by employers across Victoria, recruits qualified engineers from refugee or asylum seeker backgrounds. EPIC aims to break down barriers to paid employment in Australia and opens a talent pipeline for entry-level site engineers on major transport infrastructure projects, including level crossing removal sites across the network.

The 18-month cadetship gives participants workplace experience and an Australian qualification, building the skills needed to further their careers. The cadets receive on-the-job training, support and mentoring, while completing an accredited Graduate Certificate in Infrastructure Engineering. Here are some of their stories:

HAYAT AND IHAB'S JOURNEY FROM SYRIA AND IRAQ TO METRO

Hayat's Journey from Syria to Metro

Hayat Mnayrji is a site engineer working for the South Eastern Program Alliance on the level crossing removal project, studied Telecommunications Engineering at Damascus University in Syria, moving from city to city as the Syrian civil war began in 2011. "I studied by candlelight, under artillery shells, not knowing if I would ever have the chance to use the knowledge that I was acquiring," remarked Hayat.

In 2019, Hayat left her country and her family behind and fled to Australia with her partner, Bassam. "Syrians are social and generous, and they love people and love life. Leaving was not an easy step, but we hoped for a new life and a better future."

Hayat joined the EPIC program in hope of gaining work in Australia and has since finished with a permanent position at Metro Trains, her dream job. "Metro Trains opened its doors for my passion, and I am so proud to be working for such a supportive company," said Hayat.

"I have enjoyed learning how to operate the stations with OCS equipment and designs, and I am still excited to learn more."

Ihab's Journey from Iraq to Metro

Ihab Qassab is a site engineer working for Metropolitan Roads Program Alliance on the Level Crossing Removal project.

Originally from Iraq, Ihab fled to Australia in January 2018 with his wife and three kids, after ISIS occupied his hometown of Baghdeda in 2014. "My town was my paradise and I had never left it," shared Ihab.

"When ISIS invaded, it was chaos, there was no electricity, no water and sounds of explosions were everywhere."

Ihab said that there are many things that made his hometown special, like Palm Sunday - a special day where the whole town of Baghdeda would walk around the city, singing and praying together. "I was one of the choir members. We were singing and praying every Sunday as well as at Christmas and Easter."

While Ihab enjoys singing and sport, poetry writing is what's most important to him. "Yes, I am a poetry writer. I started writing poetry in 1997 at age 12. I now have hundreds of poems in Arabic and Syrian languages. It's the most important and enjoyable hobby of mine," he said.

Ihab came to Australia with a degree in Electrical Engineering from the University of Mosul in Iraq and believes his EPIC cadetship at Metro was his golden opportunity. "The dream came true! I am very proud to be a member of the MTM family and I am going to do my very best towards this position, making MTM values and behaviors my guide in work and in life."

Ihab's number one goal was to gain a permanent contract with Metro Trains Melbourne and has since become a permanent site engineer in the signaling field at Metropolitan Roads Program Alliance.

THE HOW

When I asked her who focuses on these outreach efforts in a practical sense she said they have a small team of "very enthusiastic, very committed" supervisors in the Passenger Experience area of the agency, who "probably sparked the fire in this diversity and inclusion space."

MTM recently had a class full of individuals that were primarily females brought in through the "socially responsible employment" route. They were recruited by word of mouth and that "small team of individuals who have access into fields where they would be able to reach out to the right groups of individuals" she says.

Tilly asserts they are also getting to be known as a business that take this approach, and therefore that breeds success of bringing people along to be interested in in being employed there. She states, "I think it is also about the processes that are in place and making sure that they're not restrictive or unnecessarily restrictive to prevent people coming in who perhaps wouldn't otherwise be able to, you know?"

One way of doing that they have pursued is not putting an assessment in place "for an assessment sake" and making sure that the hiring processes they use are tailored to know if somebody has got particular learning needs. She continues, "For instance, how do we make sure that they get the right provision? So that the hurdle of any assessment is not an unnecessary one – requiring more than the role requires once in the business. Allowing an individual to get into the business and share what they can do and shine."

EDUCATION

There are also educational efforts around the positions that are available. For instance, the Authorised Officer role is a team of individuals who are there for revenue protection, compliance ticketing but also a primary focus on customer service in the field. She asked, "How can we get people to know more about their roles? We have a small Community Engagement Unit and they created a video about what Authorised Officers do. It was aimed at schoolchildren, but it can be used for a much broader picture. With kids asking questions about you know what do you do in your role, but that type of resource? We are looking to be more creative to utilise resources then also available to show people what can you do with Metro. You know from a different angle rather than it just being the flat position description that you know isn't necessarily going to appeal to everybody."

WHERE TO START

When I asked her how agencies could start if they wanted to mirror these programs, she said, "Spend some time in looking at the community you are trying to reflect."

Tilly says Metro is in the early stages of "socially responsible hiring". She states that "it is hard work. Getting an infrastructure to ensure people are supported takes some time and energy. Some of the individuals that come in through this route do require different types and levels of support. In some instances they are not used to, or out of practice at, being in a workplace or have lots going on outside the workplace that they need to work through." She continues, "Once you've got that more diverse workforce though, and the ability to see through a different customer lens, which is effectively what it allows us to do – that is huge. The benefits that the richness of the diversity of individuals in the workforce brings is priceless."

She said they also do a lot more, generally around bringing their frontline people stories to LinkedIn and Facebook and to try and "bring that alive. There's some fantastic things that our people do on a day-to-day basis that we just don't see."

SUMMARY

Equity and Inclusion can have many meanings. In Australia for Metro Trains Melbourne it includes efforts to include long term unemployed individuals, refugees, those with physical or other disabilities and women who have suffered domestic violence into the workforce.

CHAPTER 11

DAVID KIM

Former Secretary of Transportation (California)

Hear David's statewide perspective

Paul Comfort: David could you tell us a little bit of your background?

David Kim: Sure. I'm David Kim, former secretary of the California State Transportation Agency (CALSTA). I served in that position from the summer of 2019 until January of 2022.

I stepped down and decided to return to the DC area where I lived for many, many years before going to Sacramento for the CALSTA position. Although I'm a California native, I've spent most of my adulthood in the DC area and a couple months ago I joined WSP USA and have a really long title. Let's see if I can remember it, Senior Vice President and Principal National Transportation Policy and Multimodal Strategy.

It's a long winded way of saying I'm involved in lots of different projects across all modes, transit and rail, EV charging deployment of electric vehicles, road and bridge projects. The road usage charge, which is being contemplated as the future replacement for the gas tax, is really involved in that.

So it's been great to get immersed into the world of architect and engineering firms like WSP and to be back in the DC area. So that's a little bit about my background.

Paul Comfort: Thank you. So tell us about your view on equity and inclusion and it's importance to you and what you have done and in the past that you think has been productive.

David Kim: Yeah, we made this a huge priority during my time as Secretary of CALSTA. It all started shortly after the killing of George Floyd, where we felt it necessary to put out a strong statement on equity condemning structural institutional racism and acknowledging the fact that transportation decisions of the past had a damaging impact on communities of color, and we have to own up to that. And we have to do something about it. So we put out that strong statement. I will say it was well received.

But words only go so far. It's all about actions. We have to back up those words with actions. And so we went about trying to do that during my time in Sacramento, first by looking at the workforce and making sure that we had conversations with our employees at CALSTA and all of the departments have belonged to CALSTA, like Caltrans, DMV, High Speed Rail Authority to talk about equity. What does it mean? Why is it important? What should we collectively and individually do about it? And so we had those in internal conversations and those are ongoing. I think it takes a lot of time and effort to make sure people understand it and internalize it as much as possible, to make sure it's a priority for them as well as for the agency.

And, we had employees go through training, equity diversity and inclusion training, implicit bias training, and it's a work in progress. It takes a long time to make sure that those concepts really sink in and people understand them, and then to institutionalize and to integrate them into the everyday work of transportation planning, project selection and delivery. That's a process and it's still under way, but I think we've made great strides in the first couple of years of the pandemic. I feel that we made excellent progress and there's still a long way to go to be sure. But that's what we did as a state agency. And those efforts will continue for many years to come.

Paul Comfort: So you mentioned that you integrated them into the day-to-day transportation delivery and planning. Tell us what that looked like?

David Kim: Yeah. So for example, CALSTA has a number of discretionary grant programs, including one called the transit and Intercity Rail Capital Program or TIRCP. It's a pretty large grant program of about $500 million every other year for transit agencies to use for capital purposes, to extend and expand their system. Also to purchase and acquire zero emission buses and to electrify their fleet.

And we really wanted to make sure that equity was at the center of our eligibility criteria and the factors we would look at when evaluating grant applications. So that is very much front and center in that program, and then throughout.

So on that discretionary grant program, equity is very much front and center. And same with other things like the California High Speed Rail project.

As we begin the process of station planning and development, making sure that equity is very much rooted in that work. And making sure that communities of color that are served by high speed rail can benefit from station development, planning around stations, land use planning, of course jobs and the high speed rail project has created thousands of jobs in the Central Valley of California. Which is a largely disadvantaged community suffering from air quality challenges. And it has been for many years. And so I feel that equity is very much rooted in a project, a transformational project like California High Speed Rail.

Paul Comfort: You recently wrote an interesting piece on LinkedIn where you talked about how this is implemented really in route planning of course but also in safety, which is big. Pedestrian safety is a large part of what we look at from a holistic viewpoint of transportation projects in any community, tell us about your views on that.

David Kim: It's really alarming to see trends in Road safety where fatalities and serious injuries are going up, especially among vulnerable Road users, pedestrians and bicyclists. And where are those instances happening? They are happening largely in communities of color, in communities that have seen disinvestment over the years and so, for example, in LA it's a pretty alarming statistic and I have to see if I can remember it by heart. 6% of streets in LA are responsible for something like 65% of fatalities and serious injuries. That's alarming, and the vast majority of those streets are located in communities of color. Low income communities especially Watts and West Adams. Places like that. And these are communities that lack basic infrastructure, like sidewalks.

Pedestrian crossing infrastructure, complete streets, Road diets, things of that nature are what's needed. And it's not just LA, it's everywhere around the country. I don't want to single out LA. This is a pattern everywhere. And so it shows historic under investment or disinvestment in the most basic of transportation infrastructure, especially for pedestrians. And so we've got to change that and it takes a real intentional mindset to devote. Not equate resources to reverse historic under investment or disinvestment in these kinds of neighborhoods.

And so I'm hoping, I'm hopeful that will happen in the years ahead, especially with this movement towards Vision 0, which many cities have adopted as a policy, but for the most part they have not succeeded in reducing fatalities and serious injuries. So I think as a country collectively we all have a lot of work to do to reverse that trend and get closer to where the numbers ought to be, especially when you look globally in places like Europe and Asia where the numbers are going down, the US is an outlier where the numbers are going up. And so clearly we've got to take a different approach, a more urgent approach to reducing and reversing the trend.

Paul Comfort: Yes. What other things would you suggest that statewide agencies look at as practical steps they could do to help implement more equity and inclusion, not only in their agency, but also in their grantees and in the programs they administer?

David Kim: Right. I think especially given the new infrastructure law where so much of this funding goes through state DOTs, it's really a great opportunity for states to play an important leadership role and provide guidance, best practices and encourage local recipients of federal funds to use funding to really advance the ball on all of these issues we're talking about to build more basic infrastructure and sidewalks.

It's things like protected bike lanes, crossing infrastructure, Road diets, complete streets, especially in underserved neighborhoods, and really press upon them the importance of doing so and making this a priority. And on the transit side, I think it's pretty generally well understood, but worth emphasizing that in communities that are relatively affluent and that are predominantly white, community transit generally works better there compared to lower income communities with large communities of color. And so I think as a nation, transit agencies really need to try to prioritize as much as they can the provision of bus service and transit service in underserved communities. And I do have to give a shout out to LA Metro and others because I do think transit agencies, by and large, have been thinking about equity for quite a long time before the pandemic, before George Floyd and LA Metro is a good example of that. One project I'm really excited about, which will come online later this year, is the Crenshaw Light rail project, which has been under construction for the past seven or eight years, but should be operational later this year. I'm excited because Crenshaw will serve a historically underserved community, predominantly black community and really historic neighborhoods like South LA, Inglewood, Hyde Park, Leimert Park, and it will connect to LA International Airport (LAX) and it will open up incredible opportunity for residents of South LA and surrounding neighborhoods. So I'm really excited about it. Yeah. And I think it's a great example of a transit agency thinking long and hard about how to improve service and make it equitable, especially in underserved communities.

Paul Comfort: That's wonderful. Thanks, David. Is there anything else you'd like to share on this topic?

David Kim: Yes, when it comes to zero emission buses we're seeing so many transit agencies around the country really try to accelerate the transition to electrify their fleet. And in California it's a mandate, maybe that's not the case elsewhere, but still outside of California, transit agencies are taking concerted steps to electrify their fleet. That's really exciting and we know that that's a huge investment of time and resources.

How agencies start to deploy zero emission buses. It's a great opportunity for them to figure out and think about where does it make sense to deploy these buses, zero emission buses, not just from an operational standpoint, but also from an equity standpoint?

We all know that low income communities of color have suffered the most from air quality challenges with greenhouse gas emissions.

And so what a great chance for agencies to think carefully and thoughtfully about where to deploy these buses, maybe in a place like LA, could they be deployed in South LA or Inglewood or Hyde Park? Places like W Adams, places like that to provide immediate air quality benefits to disadvantaged communities. So I think it's a great opportunity as agencies look ahead and as they plan ahead for this transition to zero emission buses.

Paul Comfort: Thanks. Anything else?

David Kim: Yes, one other thing. In addition to redesigning bus networks, I think transit agencies would do well to also think about how to add features like bus shelters. These are really basic things.

And as we all know, many lower income communities of color do not have bus shelters that will protect riders from the elements from the steaming heat and from the pouring rain. And what a great message that would send to these communities that we care about you and we want to provide for you important amenities like bus shelters and people may not think of them as significant but they are, especially in places that are really hot like the Southwest, or have harsh winters like the northeast, and so that's a really important message to riders that we care about you, and we're going to provide these basic but very important amenities to enhance and to improve your experience on our transit system.

Paul Comfort: Well, thank you. This has been very helpful with very practical ideas for statewide agencies.

CHAPTER 12

VERONICA VANTERPOOL

Deputy Administrator
US Federal Transit Administration

Veronica shares her national perspective

Paul Comfort: Veronica, tell me some about your background.

Veronica Vanterpool: I have worked for about 15 years in the transportation sector, mostly in the nonprofit sector in advocacy, working on public policy campaigns and education around sustainable transportation, including how we invest in our public transit systems and the walking and bicycle infrastructure in our communities; land use, and how those priorities are reflected in budget and policy decisions. I am new to federal government.

Paul Comfort: And what's your role as Deputy Administrator?

Veronica Vanterpool: I work with the strong leadership team here on day-to-day operations and policy priorities of the Biden-Harris Administration. This includes helping FTA execute the Administration's goals of safety, equity, climate change and economic development and providing data and examples of how FTA is meeting these goals.

I also represent FTA in other cities to highlight how FTA grant funds are being used to improve transit service or for important, exciting announcements like grant announcements or groundbreakings. For example, I was recently in Birmingham, Alabama with Secretary Buttigieg when he announced Reconnecting Communities, a new grant program that awards funds to communities previously cut off from economic opportunities by transportation infrastructure.

I also engage with our team to improve internal processes and develop tools, such as our Strategic Plan, and collaborate with other agencies within the Department of Transportation on shared goals and activities.

Paul Comfort: That's great. And tell me about this. What's the FTA and the federal government's view, role, and thoughts in the area of equity and inclusion? And what are you all hoping to do in this important area?

Veronica Vanterpool: The way we're advancing equity at the Federal Transit Administration is by ensuring that we are getting this significant, unprecedented amount of funding Congress has allocated to transit into communities by funding cleaner, greener transit vehicles and supporting transit agencies as they think about new and improved ways of getting transit users where they need and want to travel. We are also providing resources to retrain, retain and reskill a transit workforce that is experiencing a labor shortage.

FTA is investing $5 million in the first ever transit workforce center to prepare the industry from both a sustainability angle but also from a workforce angle. This also advances equity because transit is one of the greenest, most efficient, sustainable ways of getting around, especially in communities overburdened with transportation infrastructure.

On the workforce side, jobs in the transit sector are pathways to strong livelihoods. Transit is a lifeline for those without access to a vehicle, particularly those from communities of color and low-income communities.

Equity remains very front and center for us. With a budget of $20 billion, thanks to the Bipartisan Infrastructure Law, it can be said that FTA is actually making a

$20 billion dollar transit equity investment. When you make investments in transit, you're making investments in equitable communities, especially for those individuals who rely on transit or have fewer mobility options.

Paul Comfort: That's good. What have you seen in your travels and also even in your previous career, that are some best practices when it comes to public transit agencies, promoting equity inclusion in their own agency and in their communities?

Veronica Vanterpool: Exceptional public engagement is essential. Insufficient public engagement can threaten the viability of a good project. Engaging with the community about a project has to be more than just checking off a list of action items. It can be about new methods and windows of engagement: evening and weekend meetings instead of lunchtime meetings during the workweek or the provision of translation services, childcare and food.

There are many experts in government and transit agencies, but community members are experts in their communities as well. The USDOT is doing public engagement well with a team, many of whom have expertise working on the ground, focused on developing and sustaining external stakeholder relationships beyond business groups and trade associations.

Another best practice is for transit agencies to be nimble with their vision and goals and not have a fixed goal that never changes. Right now, transit agencies have to think differently about some of the service being provided or maybe some of the projects that are in the pipeline because of shifts in ridership patterns and a decline in revenue sources.

The goal should be to provide the best service possible for the community amidst changing circumstances.

Paul Comfort: Yeah, I think that's good. That's very important. A lot of times we have kind of our eye on the prize and we start pushing toward that, like a bulldog, we don't take into consideration the community input we're getting. In Baltimore, when I was CEO at the MTA there, we were trying to create a rebranding and rebuilding of all the routes in our Baltimore Link program.

We had 200 public meetings and we got so much input that we changed like half of what we were going to do based on the feedback. Sometimes our data and models said we should put the route or stop in one place, but people who use the service came out and said, "no, no, Mrs. Smith has no other option. She's got to get on the vehicle there. If you move it one street over, she'll never be able to get to her appointments". So we listened and tried to respond as best as we could.

Veronica Vanterpool: I love that example. That's wonderful to know. And, to know that you were part of that when you were a CEO.

Paul Comfort: Yes. So where do you see us going as a nation when it comes to equity and inclusion?

I think it's become a very important part of our industry right now, and transit agencies are focused on it. Like Alex Wiggins told me, down in New Orleans, he wants to see everything through the lens of equity and inclusion. And transit agencies are being used basically to help give a step up to people who've maybe traditionally been underserved.

Where do you see us going as an industry and as a nation in the overall area and the story arc of improving our equity and inclusion?

Veronica Vanterpool: Transit has always been focused on providing mobility to those individuals who need it the most. Now, that doesn't mean that there haven't been adjustments needed in how that service is provided and what the provision of that service looks like.

During the pandemic, it became more obvious to transit agencies that there are groups of people not being well served by transit. It exposed the inordinate focus given to delivering service to the 9 to 5 weekday commuter, for example.

To advance equity and inclusion, the transit industry must dynamically respond to shifting travel patterns and adapt. For instance, people are not just traveling into city centers anymore; they are reverse commuting to the suburbs or within the city/community in which they live. Weekend service is also rivaling weekday service—a new pattern that requires a shift in service frequency and availability on the weekends.

In short, the lesson learned is to be flexible and nimble to best respond to shifting patterns.

New research suggests people will still be commuting in person on transit systems, but instead of doing so Monday – Friday, they will shift commuting to Tuesdays, Wednesdays and Thursdays. What happens to Monday and Friday service? Is service reduced, and for whom? The future of equity and inclusion requires flexibility to respond to changing and emerging mobility needs because the type of service people need in the next year or two might significantly change again in five years as systems return to pre pandemic ridership levels. Then, the industry might be responding again to buses and trains being beyond capacity; what do we need to do then? Flexibility is key.

Paul Comfort: That's good. That's a great message. I guess my last big question would be about having come from the role of an advocate and now working in government and being inside the organization you were advocating to. What is your message to other advocates in the community who are pushing for just what you're talking about?

Veronica Vanterpool: Use solid data and create opportunities for people to connect with the issue. Good data helps develop a winning narrative. It's also important to make connections to the work.

Bring elected officials and policymakers to the streets to see and witness some of the challenges and needs There's no written substitute to sitting at a street corner of a nearby school and watching cars speed above the speed limit, to make a case for why Vision Zero or Complete Streets measures are important. Or, traveling on the bus and sitting in traffic because of the lack of dedicated bus lanes to whiz through gridlock.

Now that I'm on the inside, I advocate differently. Sometimes when you're an advocate, you have to be assertive because you are trying to change opinions of a constituency of individuals often not well versed on a given issue or which may not agree. Sometimes that can be adversarial. Sometimes it's just a healthy debate on both sides until you come to a point of understanding, but I don't have to be as aggressive on the inside because I'm working with like-minded people working toward the same goals rooted in a shared value-system.

Paul Comfort: That's great. Thanks for this overview for advocates and from a national level. It's been very helpful.

CHAPTER 13

PAUL COMFORT

Transit Evangelist & Best-Selling Author

Micro Transit's Role in Creating More
Equity & Inclusion in Public Transportation

PAUL TALKS ABOUT ENSURING THAT PEOPLE DON'T GET LEFT BEHIND.

The Coronavirus Pandemic has been a crisis to public transit that is existential. Time to re-examine why we exist. Is it just to provide the fastest connection from A to B for the masses rushing to work? No. It is also to provide access to life's opportunities for all.

Up until recently most transit agencies and governments felt public transit's number one goal or key performance indicator (KPI) was ridership. That was how we determined if we were successful. That is why in 2017-2019 there was such a push to increase ridership after a long spell of declining ridership – following the "Houston" model. Houston Metro was the first US agency to turn around ridership numbers in 2016 followed by seven more in 2017, many more in 2018 and finally the whole industry, including New York City, in 2019.

The Coronavirus pandemic put a halt to rising ridership as passenger counts plummeted 50-95% globally. Following the successful Houston model, agencies now began to again re-evaluate ridership trends to determine what type of routes and service levels we should re-emerge from this pandemic with to meet the needs of today/tomorrow's passengers.

As part of this re-evaluation, agencies/governments are also evaluating how ridership patterns for commuter trains and buses continue to be much lower than pre pandemic levels. Most saw ridership plunge over 90% and now with lower peak demand for the foreseeable future, because major businesses in downtowns are remaining in hybrid mode and not returning to office 5 days a week, many have spread their trains throughout the day and moved to more of a regional rail service, offering more mid-day, nights and weekend service.

During the pandemic, public transit existed primarily to provide mobility for our essential workers and ridership levels in most cities remained around 50% for core bus service as a result. Transit, it turns out is not just for "choice" commuters hustling to their "9 to 5" jobs in the big tall buildings downtown. It actually has proven to be the backbone of our economy because it provides mobility and access for employees to the key jobs that are required for our economy and society to properly function - like grocery store clerks/pharmacy techs "critical retail", energy/infrastructure workers, first responders/medical staff, agriculture/food production, transportation/warehouse/ delivery and the like,

So, if public transportation isn't only to serve the "mass transit" needs of white-collar commuters but also to underpin the mobility needs of the front line workers running our daily economy/society, then it appears our overarching key performance indicator of ridership may not be the only KPI that determines success.

It has become clear to most that public transit does not primarily exist to provide mass transportation for commuters but also to provide mobility access for all people to all of life's opportunities. **We exist to provide mobility for all. That is our "raison d'etre" or reason to exist.**

OUR "ALTERS" TO HIGHER RIDERSHIP HAVE FALLEN.

Based on the fall 2020 American Public Transportation Association (APTA) Transit Agency Survey – Transit Agencies have re-ordered their priorities with ridership now no longer the top Key Performance Indicator (KPI) as follows:

1. Customer Satisfaction
2. Ridership
3. Access to Mobility Options

The recent successful US based model to reboot our bus networks (from 2016-2019) can continue to be useful as agencies phase out of the Covid Pandemic into a new normal. This could be a template that can continue to work with some modification as follows:

1. Analyze and determine highest ridership times and routes and provide bus route networks that meet that need. Many routes were laid out years ago with the heaviest concentrations in the central business district but now that businesses have located outside the central business district these routes need to be reconfigured to take people where the jobs and trip drivers are today. Additionally, due to hybrid work schedules, many commuters are using transit less frequently and at different times of the day for meetings but not necessarily to work at their office all day.

2. Setting up standards for bus routes and stops that require certain levels of productivity to utilize a 40 foot bus to service them on a regular basis. Removing routes and stops that don't meet these standards to adequately shepherd resources.

3. Add frequency to the routes where most people want to ride at 10-15 minute headways.

4. Add in bus only lanes, transit signal priority and good vehicle tracking, boarding/faring policies to improve the overall speed-Mph of the service and make it more efficient. Giving the buses priority means they don't get stuck in the same rush-hour traffic as cars and it makes them more attractive as a faster and more convenient mobility solution.

5. Integrate the various modes of mobility in a city to allow for more effective transfers between light rail, subway, regional rail, bus and micro mobility. Bus routes can be modified to link them all together with passenger protection and reliable real time rider info on cell phones, platforms and vehicles to ensure that transfers can be effectively made.

Then blending in the new raison d'etre (reason to exist) – to help people access all of life's opportunities – these additional steps can be taken -

6. Now look at your system through the lens of equity and see where the gaps in service are. Have routes or stops been moved away from communities of color/lower income/elderly passengers to meet productivity standards? Has this impacted people that really need this service for mobility and have few other options?

7. Similar to how the Americans with Disabilities Act (ADA) made public transportation a civil right for people with disabilities, the most vulnerable actually need public transportation more than the less vulnerable who have other options. To ensure equity and inclusion agencies should make sure that groups that may have been marginalized in transit route planning in the past do not get disenfranchised with these service changes.

8. Providing mobility on demand (MOD)/ micro transit fills these gaps to ensure that no one is left behind. Areas with little to no regular mass transit service and not enough passenger demand to justify 40' bus regular route service can be placed in MOD zones so that passengers there can have access to public mobility. They can call or use a smartphone app to plan, book and pay for their trip seamlessly. And this mobility on demand service does not have to clog our streets unnecessarily with individual trips in cars by using a shared ride model, with back office software that includes powerful algorithms to determine the best pick up time and location to allow for multiple passengers and maximize trip productivity (rides per hour) balanced with on-time performance.

Using Microtransit/Mobility on Demand (MOD) as a layer on top of rebooted bus/ rail networks ensures access to mobility options for all, ensuring no one is left behind and that there is equity and inclusion. Thus microtransit/MOD can be a sort of safety net during these route rebalancing efforts and expanding service into transit deserts.

DELAWARE

The transit system in Delaware is a good example of how this works. In April 2021, the Delaware Transit Corporation, which provides public transportation under the DART brand, launched its microtransit DART Connect in Georgetown and Millsboro, Delaware. The on-demand zones in these towns provide twice as many people a convenient connection to transit within a quarter mile of their home than the previous deviated fixed route system it replaced – 6,978 versus 3,449. The doubling of the service area population did not significantly change the percentage of persons served of low-income (21.5%) or minority (45.0%) status, indicating the strong need for broadening access to transit, a need which can be met with microtransit in areas that can't be served well by fixed route transit, such as rural areas.

The need for more accessible transit was demonstrated by other indicators: Georgetown is designated an Opportunity Zone, the town's percentage of rental housing is 25 percentage points higher than the state as a whole, and the car-light population (zero or one car households) is 10 percentage points higher.

Completely on-demand, DART Connect can be booked either by app or phone, with the service seeing about half app, half call booked trips, indicative of the technology divide that will be an initial limiter in widespread deployments of microtransit. DART Connect ensures people, no matter where they live in the on-demand zone, have equitable access to quality transit services, including four fixed route services that provide statewide accessibility.

As John Sisson, the CEO of DART said, "In Delaware, we start with the foundation that Mobility is a Right and work tirelessly to provide everyone with a safe and efficient transportation network. Our DART Connect microtransit service is latest tool that we have at our disposal to help make connections, particularly in areas without good pedestrian infrastructure or the density to support traditional fixed route service."

In Delaware and numerous other locations around the country, this new enhanced model of microtransit allows public transportation to meet its overall goals efficiently and helps our communities achieve more equity and inclusion.

SACRAMENTO

Although microtransit mimics popular ride-hailing services, it's much more affordable appealing to a diverse and all-inclusive customer-base. Affordability and equitability are some of the best features of microtransit service – For example, in the Sacramento, California region, Sacramento Regional Transit (SacRT) has been able to keep the cost low by using existing resources and grant funding to operate the service in nine zones to become one of the largest and most successful microtransit services in the nation. Customers only pay SacRT's fixed-route fare, including discounted rates for seniors and persons with disabilities, and free for youth in grades kindergarten through 12th as part of SacRT's trailblazing RydeFreeRT fare-free for students program. As Henry Li, the General Manager/CEO of SacRT said, "microtransit goes a long way to make public transit relevant in a fast-paced, technology driven world while ensuring the barrier of residential isolation is eliminated, advancing access to jobs, education, healthcare and other vital resources."

CHAPTER 14

AMERICAN PUBLIC TRANSPORTATION ASSOCIATION (APTA)

Equity & Inclusion Programs

APTA, the largest transit industry association in America has been in the forefront of efforts to lead on improving equity and inclusion in public transportation. I recently spoke with three key leaders of the association on that topic:

Petra Mollet - Vice-President Strategic and international Programs
Linda Ford – General Counsel
TJ Doyle - Vice President, Communications and Marketing

Petra Mollet: One of the things I think that we have really been seeing, especially in the last year and a half is that public transit is a big factor in providing equity and community. Much like I would say previously of sustainability, right? We've always been a factor in being a great greening of our communities, but we never really laid it out until maybe 10, 15 years ago and really started the effort.

A year and a half ago there was this call for us to say, we can do better. We can do more. And, and we can talk about what we're doing and we can measure what we're doing and we can be very intentional. And I think that's really what has shifted in the last year and a half, both with the transit industry and as APTA itself.

We had a diversity and inclusion strategic plan from 2017 onwards, but it was a call really from our chair then Nuria Fernandez to say, we must do more. And, and we have to be very explicit and intentional.

So that's when we started an effort to bring our members together, from the business members, as well as the agency side to create a racial equity working group. We talked about racial equity at the forefront with the view that it is intersectional. If you're focusing on racial equity you really are focusing on equity for all.

We developed a racial equity action plan, which really lays out what can we, as an association collectively do with our members to ensure that we are advancing equity in both our organizations, which is needed if we're going to advance it in the community. So the second thing I would say here is that I think agencies as well as business members have also decided to be more intentional and really look at everything they're doing in their own agencies and in their communities to ensure that it truly is an equity improver and not something that that that is making the situation worse or is just leaving some people disenfranchised.

But they're realizing they have to walk the walk internally. They have to be focused on diversity inclusion and belonging internally for them to be in a position to also focus on what they're doing with their customers in their community. And I think that that also has shifted. So the racial equity action plan really takes account of that and lays out a number of areas that we felt we could make a real difference in with regard to APTA.

Linda Ford: I think the only thing I'd add on to that is I think the racial equity action plan is it comes out of the fact that as transit professionals were, we weren't immune to the Black Lives Matter Movement. We weren't immune to the pain of watching George Floyd being killed or Brianna Taylor and all those other atrocities. And so I think as a Transit industry we looked around and we say, we serve brown communities, communities of color, and what can we do to better support and be reflective and supportive?

And I think Patria is exactly right. I think you have to look internally first before you can kind of spread that message to your communities. And so that's where I think the commitment pilot program came into being.

The program itself is a two-year pilot program that we launched obviously at the Transform Conference. And we're asking folks to sign up soon. If you don't mind, I'll just read, the five core principle of the program:

The action plan outlines five key goals and accompanying areas for action:

1. Measure and recognize progress on racial equity in the transit industry, providing APTA members with a tangible roadmap for advancing racial

equity as part of a comprehensive equity framework within and for their organizations;

2. Offer the necessary training, technical support and resources to individuals and member organizations to develop practices, policies and programs that support racial justice and equity;

3. Create more mentorship, sponsorship and engagement opportunities for transit students, transit professionals and transit businesses;

4. Be a more influential advocacy force for equity and transit, promoting inclusion and diversity in the composition of executive leadership at transit agencies, the businesses that provide transit-related goods and services and their respective board of directors and equity in the delivery of transit-related goods and services, and;

5. Implement impact-oriented partnerships with organizations dedicated to equity, diversity and inclusion that is supportive of the goals and mission of APTA and its Racial Equity Action Plan.

So the plan itself includes definitions of the goals of the pilot program, as well as a year one and year two milestones that include reporting out to APTA on how you're doing, meeting your milestones, any challenges that you have, and anything that's working really well, because we certainly do want to collect that.

And then also it acts as a commitment to taking information collected during the two year program and coming out with a report on what we saw during the pilot program, and then officially launching it much the way we have a sustainability program.

Similar to that, we would have an official launch where we would then as an organization, recognize those transit systems and businesses that are doing particularly well.

Petra Mollet: I might just add Paul, as we get going, you'll see, we're very passionate about this. The racial equity commitment pilot program is really laid out to make sure that it meets members where they're at. In the last year and a half we've seen that agencies and business members are all at different places in their journey on diversity, equity and inclusion. And we just want to make sure at APTA that we're providing the necessary tools and resources for our members to access.

And it's not just us saying here, here are the things you must do. Or here, here are tools or resources. It's also about creating this collective learning environment. We realized how important it is for the members of the transit industry to be really speaking with each other about this.

And, and as Linda pointed out, this is as much about, "Hey, what's working? As much as it is about, well these are challenging things that we came across and this is not working." So it really is a bit sort of creating that continuous improvement process. It's not about if you do these five things, you're good, you're an equitable system. We hope it just helps our members along in that journey if they've committed to doing so.

I also wanted to mention the commitment of program is one of the key elements of this racial equity action plan, but there are other areas we are focusing on as well. You may have noticed our Kaleidoscope webinars series, which we kicked off in this year. Again, that is really to give people an insight on what are agencies doing. It's really that boots on the ground. I think your book will be a good compliment to this program.

I would also say look at our diversity equity inclusion hub on the APTA website. If you go to About APTA, you'll see diversity equity inclusion, that's got everything there. It's got a racial equity action plan. It's got a section on the commitment as well and also a list of actions that agencies and business members have taken so far. (Here's a link: https://www.apta.com/research-technical-resources/diversity-equity-and-inclusion/)

Petra Mollet: And Paul the other area we are very much focused on is our workforce development. We know there's a big disconnect between the leadership and the frontline workforce in terms of being reflective of the communities that we serve. And that's certainly something that we're looking at and very attuned to, and also ensuring that we attract talent from diverse communities to be a part of the transit workforce.

The other part we're looking at as well is in teaching. TJ, you may be able to talk a little bit more about that as well, but just in our advocacy efforts we're also making sure that we talk about the role of transit, very intentionally in terms of equity. And that we ensure as part of our work at APTA that we are reaching out to communities that don't normally have a voice locally in terms of transit.

TJ Doyle: So that would be our voices for public transit. Digital grassroots advocacy. And they have been a vital part in voice for us throughout the pandemic, throughout the investment conversation.

But in particular, this is a group of, you know, Joe and Jane Smith around the country who care about transit for a reason, aside from us advocating on the Capitol Hill for the equity conversation and for the climate conversation. I would say overall, that this is as much a listening exercise, as it is a communicating out exercise.

And throughout this process, the inputs we get, it's our goal to then amplify what our systems are doing in any variety of ways. So, whether it would be our own podcast or a commentary on our passenger transport, or just highlighting it on social media. Like what's happening in Pinellas County, Florida, Chicago or any of these other good examples.

You know, we have a webinar series. We're just trying to make sure that our members are hearing and seeing what others are doing. And then as we get more inputs, we can then further build out that level of communication. So, in a nutshell, this is just tip of the iceberg.

Petra Mollet: And Paul, last but not least, I would also say, you know, none of this happens in silos, right?

So APTA is working closely in partnership with other organizations like COMTO (Conference of Minority Transportation Officials), Latinos in Transit, WTS (Women Transportation Seminar). These are very important partners in this work.

PUBLIC TRANSPORTATION INDUSTRY LEADERS

Public Transportation is supported by a large number of industries that provide all the supplies and services needed to run the services. Many of these businesses have taken leadership roles in the fight to improve equity and inclusion in public transportation.

As one such leader Rob Desanti, General Manager of Transit for TripSpark Technologies said, "We're excited about the industry-wide focus on equity and inclusion and what it means for expanding transportation flexibility, particularly for paratransit riders. Today with many paratransit services, the ability to make impromptu plans can be difficult, and the feedback we've received from our customers has been that "spontaneity is key" to inclusion. It is our mission, and specialty, to enable robust paratransit operations and expand on them for general public on-demand services."

Other companies have also stepped up and made commitments and are carrying out this mission of improving equity and inclusion in our industry and in their companies. Here's some comments from Teresa Domingo, General Manager of Trapeze Group, where I have been employed for the past five years,

"Transit Agencies' core mission is to provide mobility and access to opportunity for all. Palm Tran's mission is to provide access to opportunity for everyone; safely, efficiently, and courteously. Terry White, General Manager of King County Metro, speaks about transit taking you "from a place to a place". The power behind this statement is "a place" in one's life is more than simply a location. We've heard transit be referred to as the great equalizer through providing mobility and access to opportunity for all. Delivering on the core mission of transit agencies promotes Diversity, Equity, and Inclusion.

At Trapeze Group, we exist to empower movement through life. We enable transit agencies by delivering best-in-class public transportation software solutions that help them achieve their goals, like rider experience or operational efficiencies. While we aren't providing mobility and access to opportunity with our software solutions, we are putting transit agencies in a position where they can deliver on their core mission. Very similarly, at Trapeze Group, we are proud to promote a culture that supports Diversity, Equity, and Inclusion.

There are countless studies nowadays, supported by data, which indicate companies with a diverse and inclusive workplace experience higher revenue growth, greater readiness to innovate, greater chance of maintaining a diverse talent pool, and have higher employee retention. Over the last 15 years at Trapeze Group, we've seen a significant shift in diversity. Most recently, our senior leadership team has reached a 50/50 split between men and women. Furthermore, we have representation from many cultures and varying experiences that sit at our senior leadership table while fostering a strong culture of transparency, challenge, and support. Consequently, we're innovating more than we have and are driving towards stronger growth than we've seen in the past 5 years for our business.

People want to be a part of a culture that is aligned with their values. We have programs in place at Trapeze Group to support Diversity, Equity and Inclusion and the response has been high, giving us an indication that it's positive for our employees. We conduct training, social events, have intentional conversations and we are continuously asking for feedback around Diversity, Equity, and Inclusion. We are working on removing biases in the workplace from hiring to promoting and recognizing that our work is never done; we can always do more. If we have a place to work where people feel like they belong, we believe we are in an excellent position to grow a healthy and strong business that supports our customers, the top 200 largest transit agencies across North America, deliver on their core missions."

Peter Aczel, GM of transit tech company Vontas asserts, ""Equity and accessibility have played a significant role in public transit for quite some time, but in the post - COVID -19 pandemic world, it has become a major focus for agencies and riders everywhere. As a technology solution provider for public transit, we have a responsibility to deliver solutions to empower our customers, the operators, to offer highly inclusive services. We strive to meet this goal through technology solutions that help them quickly adapt to the evolving needs of their communities while effectively managing their human and material assets. In addition, these tools allow public transit agencies to tailor their services to give the most vulnerable in our communities access to jobs, education, healthcare, and other essential services."

Now read chapters from three key companies with in depth discussions on what they are doing now to promote equity and inclusion in their companies and our industry.

PUBLIC TRANSPORTATION INDUSTRY BUSINESS LEADERS

NORA KAMAL

Organizational Development Manager
Proterra, Inc.

Here is what Proterra (electric bus and battery manufacturer) is doing....

Nora Kamal: Within society, there was a huge movement for racial equity and inclusion in 2020.

Proterra took a strong stance to be supportive of the racial equity movement and to make sure that the company is diverse, it's equitable, and it's inclusive of everyone.

Last year, I believe it was towards the end of June, we launched our OneProterra initiative with our three DEI committees. I like to call them our three pillars that we aim to uphold at Proterra. Our Workplace Committee focuses on everything that involves our workplace, so think about it from being what we do that is internally focused to ensure that we are being equitable and inclusive of everyone.

Our second pillar is the Workforce Committee, which focuses on how we are attracting diverse populations to Proterra, and once we bring them in, then looking at our practices around promotions, training development, to ensure they are fair and equitable.

The third pillar is our Industries and Communities Committee, which focuses on our external-facing work - making sure that we're getting into our communities to make a difference to better support the diverse communities that we serve, whether that be getting out and volunteering, building awareness and education, or promoting racial equity in our industry

I was hired on at the beginning of January 2021, as the Organizational Development Manager. Part of my role was focusing on training and development for our employees, career pathing, performance management, etc. all the things that typically fall under organizational development, but I was also given the amazing opportunity to lead our DEI initiatives for Proterra and being able to ensure that we are constantly working towards a workplace that is inclusive and equitable of everyone.

Our committees meet regularly to collaborate on various initiatives to drive positive changes. I also try to stay included in our employee affinity groups to see what they're doing, make sure they have what they need to come together, and keep a connection between our affinity groups and our committees.

Paul Comfort: What kind of affinity groups are there?

Nora Kamal: Our Women of Proterra affinity group is very, very active. We have other groups including Latinx at Proterra, and Southeast Asians at Proterra.

Paul Comfort: Are these groups that the employees started themselves and you kind of work with them to make sure they have any corporate support they need?

Nora Kamal: Correct. Yep.

Take Women of Proterra. This year alone, I can't even count the number of different activities they had.

They had a wonderful speaker series where they invited women leaders from other organizations to come and talk at Proterra about how they got to where they are in their careers, what they've been working on in their current roles, and how important it was to have had mentors to help support them along the way.

We also had a wonderful leadership webinar featuring women leaders of Proterra come and talk about how they got to this point in their careers, challenges they had to overcome, and to give general advice to other women of Proterra.

They've had a lot of support from leadership and other employees around the organization, which is extremely important.

It's not just women that are part of the group. There are a lot of men, gender non-conforming and non-binary team members, come and support the women.

We are making very strong efforts in terms of hiring diverse populations, even with our internship program.

We are making sure that we're reaching out to underrepresented groups and when we post jobs we are making concerted efforts to go out and actually reach those populations, say, hey, we have positions available.

So, for instance, as I mentioned we try to make every effort to focus on how and where we are posting our intern and co-op positions, so we not only post them on our career website and on the various university career sites but we try to reach out to specific underrepresented student groups at every university that we have a partnership with to also post our positions and share it with their members

Also, we're actually announcing this month to our employees that Proterra has become a sponsor of Latinos in Transit.

I know we have made progress, and there is still so much we can do. So, every initiative we set out to accomplish whether it is something that we do in the committees or within our workplace, we just want to make a positive impact. We want it to be an actionable effort and to actually make a difference. We're working hard around that and we want it to be meaningful. Everything we do, we want it to be intentional and meaningful because that is the only way we will truly see change.

Take our industries and communities committee. Something that we worked on this year was actually creating a diversity calendar that we share with employees and post up so that employees can see the various holidays that we try to highlight each month.

Here in Greenville, in January we worked with Greenlink to sponsor a free fare day for Rosa Parks' birthday, which is also Transit Equity Day. We wanted to showcase not only the importance of having accessible transit options for society and the impact that it can make but also the efforts that Rosa Parks made during the Civil Rights movement. So, again our committees want to make sure that when we highlight a holiday we bring awareness but also try to make an effort to do something that does something good within the community and make a difference.

In October, there are around four different holidays that were being celebrated or highlighted for the month. So we're trying to do things in our community, but also in the workplace as well, to highlight those and bring education and awareness why these days are important to those celebrating.

Paul Comfort: What else are you doing in this space?

Nora Kamal: Another thing that our workplace committee is currently working on right now is launching our DEI newsletter.

We have a beautiful newsletter that we're going to hopefully share out every month. It will highlight a variety of things such as holidays that are coming up for the month, podcasts or books that we feel like are important to share with employees to help bring about more awareness & education, we'll have an employee spotlight where we highlight a specific employee that is doing something in the community, and even a recipe corner.

Paul Comfort: That's cool.

Nora Kamal: I'm really excited to see what employees are going to be able to share because I think that that's going to build our relationships within Proterra and the of inclusivity here. We, as a company, want to make sure that we see everybody as their individual unique selves and make everyone feel comfortable to share those stories with everyone.

I do think it's going to bring us closer as a company too, so I'm excited!

Paul Comfort: How does an employee get on these committees?

Nora Kamal: We do a couple of things to spread the word about our committees. Every few months, I try to send out an email blast letting employees know to reach out if they are interested to join our committees, we also have flyers posted that talk about the work our committees are doing, as well as we will continue to highlight it in our newsletter each month

We're doing some great things and want as many employees that would like to take part to join our committees. Additionally, we talk about it in new hire orientation so that every employee that joins knows about the work we are doing and inviting them to participate. As employees are coming on board, there are slides that talk about our affinity groups and our three committees. So when employees first start, they understand the importance of DEI at Proterra and how they can make a difference if they want to join in one of the committees.

Paul Comfort: That's great. And do you have a lot of participation? How often do they meet?

Nora Kamal: We do. Each of the committees has two executive sponsors, so we have leadership sponsor those committees. Each group meets every two weeks. It's either 30 minutes or an hour, depending on what we have to talk about and projects we are working on.

But essentially, our committees are open for all employees. Regardless of where you are within the organization, if you are on the production floor, all the way up to the CEO level, anybody can join and everybody's able to participate and give ideas advice.

Paul Comfort: And have you attended all those are most of them.

Nora Kamal: Yes, I do facilitate the meetings, so I attend all of them.

Paul Comfort: And are they in-person or you've been meeting virtually because of the pandemic.

Nora Kamal: Virtually. If we have employees that are onsite, they can go to one of our meeting rooms and just log in through zoom. But I want to make sure that with that we do it virtually so that regardless of a location, including our remote population, they can always join in the call.

Paul Comfort: That's good. And, and what are some of the results you're seeing?

Nora Kamal: We have been keeping track of certain metrics internally to see where we are and if we have seen improvements from a diversity and inclusion standpoint, such as our population looking at our gender and ethnicity makeup or in our hiring, retention and promotions across the organization.

Paul Comfort: On the workplace committee, you said that they work on policies and processes you mentioned and that they have a newsletter, but are there any other activities you can tell me about that they've been working on to change policies or procedures?

Nora Kamal: A big thing we're working on is interview training to go along with a new interview process that we are currently piloting. We created a solid interview guide for hiring managers to make sure that in terms of interviewing, we're being fair and equitable.

The expectation is that anybody that's going to be an interviewer, has to go through interview training before they're able to actually interview. We're trying to get more processes in place to make sure that it is fair and it reduces unconscious biases that can come into play during interviewing and brining awareness to our teams around the unconscious biases that we all have.

Paul Comfort: Do you have committees to do interviews for people?

Nora Kamal: Yeah. We do have panels for many positions and we are working on creating a standardized process as part of this interview process to help with that.

We just want to make sure that there are clear steps within the hiring process that everybody needs to follow to make sure that we're limiting bias. We're going to hopefully keep adding to it and make improvements to our process to help ensure we have a fair process.

Paul Comfort: Any other examples of the committees reaching out to the communities? Anything else you'd like to highlight?

Nora Kamal: Yeah. For Pride Month, we actually found a company called Transit Supply in San Francisco. They make a lot of transit-oriented items and they make really cool t-shirts for Pride Month that have buses on them. They designed these really cool looking buses with like big eyes and smiles on them and has different flags that, highlight the different groups in LGBTQ+ community.

So we actually partnered together to create a Proterra Powered by Pride t-shirt. It has a bus and a bolt of lightning in the middle with the different colors of all the different flags. All the proceeds from that went to help local organizations, I believe in the San Francisco area to help support the LGBTQ+ community.

We actually had quite a number of employees buy the t-shirts, to support it and they were very excited to wear them and support the LGBTQ+ community. I believe there was about ~$2400 made from all the t-shirts that were sold.

For Hispanic heritage month, we are actually highlighting some employees -they're recording videos now and we're going to merge it together and share it on social media highlighting some of our employees that have been with Proterra and what the month means to them and how they're celebrating.

Paul Comfort: So in addition to the committees and your efforts kind of guiding the committee are there any other things outside of the committees that you can tell us about in your DEI efforts?

Nora Kamal: We want our employees to be the driving force. We are nothing without our employees and our employees are changing the world, not just with our products, but with everything they want to accomplish.

One big push of things to do within the industries and communities committee has been talking about STEM to students and giving them ideas of different careers that are pretty cool, especially in the transit space because we have seen that students kind of shy away from, especially in low-income schools.

We are looking at different partnerships in that sense. COVID kind of hit us hard with getting out in the communities and being more hands-on but we are working on finding ways that we can do that safely.

Paul Comfort: STEM is great. So what suggestions do you have for other companies in this area?

Nora Kamal: Honestly, like I will say it can seem overwhelming of where to start, right? There are so many ideas and so many things other companies are doing, and you kind of look around and think where to begin. This is something that our committees talked about. As I mentioned earlier our goal is to always make an impact with what we are doing and be very intentional.

I tend to look at it as if you're, if you're doing it slow and steady, you're making positive changes. And that's what we want to do with our, with our committees, right.

We are still early in our journey and we're not going to get it right every time we're, we're going to make mistakes, but we are going to learn and grow from them. But again, we want to do it at the right pace for our organization so that it's creating lasting change.

I think there's always going to be new ideas out there that come up and we would love to do, so keeping a list of ideas, projects, etc. is key for us. Keep that running list of things that you want to accomplish, but be mindful of what resources you have and the support you have and start from there. I think something that a lot of people need to remember and realize is that changing a culture to be more inclusive and equitable and diverse is going to take time.

Paul Comfort: Kind of like the end goal of what you're shooting for?

Nora Kamal: Yes, that is correct. Having that end goal in mind is extremely important in keeping us on track.

BRIDGETTE BEATO

Chief Executive Officer
Lumenor Consulting Group

Listen to Bridgette….

Paul Comfort: All right. So I'm with Bridgette Beato, who is CEO of Lumenor Consulting. Tell me a little about yourself and the company you lead.

Bridgette Beato: Sure. Thanks, Paul. I'm the CEO and founder of Lumenor Consulting Group, a certified DBE (Disadvantaged Business Enterprise) with offices in Alpharetta, Georgia, Jacksonville, FL, New York, NY, Philadelphia, PA and Washington, DC. I founded the company in 2007, so we're getting into our 15th year. We provide strategic advisory services to public transit agencies and other government and private sector organizations whose operations include a significant transportation component.

Paul Comfort: Okay, great, so let's start with what it's like to be a woman-owned business in the transportation industry.

Bridgette Beato: Well, I can you tell that when I started, in 2007, women-owned businesses made up approximately 36% percent of all businesses in America, now it's up to 39%. So more equitable representation is a challenge that obviously cuts across a lot of industries, but I think it's especially true for the public transit industry.

At the same time, what's also important to realize is that the public transit industry has its own issues for any new company. It's an industry where until recently the technology had not changed a lot, and where, obviously, big government agencies play a major role. So you've got relationships that go back decades, and the projects happen on a scale where there's an obvious rationale to go with well-established companies that have a visible track record. It's an environment that's extremely difficult for any newcomer to enter. And then if you're a woman, multiply that by, I don't know, 100. Then add ten, because some of the biases and obstacles you face will be even bigger than you anticipated.

But here's the thing: Diversifying our industry is an incredibly important mandate. From a strategic perspective. An economic perspective. Even before COVID, public transit ridership numbers across the country were in decline, in the face of more and more transportation. So we're an industry that needs to modernize, needs to innovate, needs to think in new ways. That means we need new players, and new pathways that can effectively bring them into our industry. And that's a big part of why things like the DBE Program are so important to our industry's future growth, sustainability, and relevance.

Paul Comfort: Okay, so let's go into a little more detail on what DBEs, or Disadvantaged Business Enterprises, are. Basically, this is a program that is designed to give businesses that are majority-owned by individuals who are "socially or economically disadvantaged," like women, or people of color, or various other groups that qualify, an "equal opportunity to receive and participate in Department of Transportation (DOT) assisted contracts."

Bridgette Beato: And these businesses who qualify are also capped in terms of size, their annual revenue limits.

Paul Comfort: Right. And what the program entails is, the state DOTs establish specific "goals" for DBE participation on a given project. For example, if a state DOT gets federal funds for a transportation project, it might establish that 12.5 percent of the overall contract value will go to DBEs?

Bridgette Beato: In theory, yes. In practice, well, we'll get to that. But first, let me just say that when I started Lumenor, we didn't have any certifications. Instead, I just went out and competed. I looked for projects that were similar to ones I had worked on as a consultant before starting my own firm and submitted proposals to agencies across the country. At that point, we only had two full-time employees and we were going up against big A&E firms (Architectural, Engineering, and Design), and some of the larger technology firms. So it was tough, but eventually in 2010, LA Metro awarded us a contract to create a Strategic Technology Plan for the Freeway Safety Patrol. And they were actually the one that said, "Hey, can you get certified?" Because they wanted to fulfill their DBE goal for that project. So that's what prompted me.

Paul Comfort: And once you had the certification, how did things change for you?

Bridgette Beato: Okay, so let me first just add a little more context here. As you know, when the DBE program started in the 1980s, the set-asides were mandatory. In the 1990s, that changed, after a Supreme Court ruling. Now, the set-asides are "goals" for some procurements. A prime contractor is supposed to make "good faith efforts" to find DBEs capable of doing work that materially contributes to the project. But all they have to do is look. They're not required to retain a DBE, even when specific goals have been set for a project on some procurements. If they make at least some documented effort to show that they tried to find a DBE, that's enough. They're allowed to hire a non-DBE sub-contractor or just do the work themselves.

So the way this plays out over time, it gets a little complicated, right? The goal is to help women, people of color, and other groups who've faced past discrimination in the system, get more equity in the industry. And to a certain extent, there's definitely progress you can point to on that front.

But even though there's this program in place, the DBE Program, which is designed to expand the industry's diversity and support and promote equity and inclusion, there are still a lot of challenges that DBEs face that arise out of how the DBE Program actually operates in the real world.

In other words, the fact that the Program exists, that it spells out these various goals and policies and gives guidance on some of the issues in play, that's a good starting point. But that's all it is too – just a starting point. Because execution matters. Enforcement matters. And then also just having an ongoing dialogue about, okay, in what ways is the Program working? Where are the pain points and how do we address them? Because to truly achieve the kind of equity that the DBE Program aims for, there needs to be stronger policies and commitments throughout the entire life-cycle of projects.

Paul Comfort: Okay, so yes, give me an example of, let's say, a grey area in the process – where DBEs face a challenge that either isn't really addressed in the Program or maybe even arises out of actual policies?

Bridgette Beato: One example involves insurance. What happens is these federal agencies are doing major projects, so they're looking to work with contractors who have really big insurance policies to cover any liabilities or other kind of damages that could happen during the course of a project. So, you know, some of the really big construction companies, they've got $5 billion policies. $10 billion policies.

And so the agencies, that's what their expectation is: If you're working on a project, they expect that you'll be carrying a pretty significant policy. But if you're a small company – and especially a small company that's just starting out – that's probably impossible.

To give you an idea of what I mean, I remember one project from our early years. The part of the contract we were going for was $500,000, that's the maximum we'd get paid for doing our part of the work. But the agency wanted us to carry an insurance policy for $5 million.

When I tried to get coverage, the brokers I spoke with told me they couldn't grant a policy that exceeded the value of the actual contract by so much. In fact, $5 million was actually more than twice my firm's annual revenues at the time!

Paul Comfort: So a classic Catch-22 more or less?

Bridgette Beato: Exactly. We couldn't get bigger unless we had the required insurance policy. But we couldn't the get required policy until we were bigger.

Paul Comfort: But were you able to overcame that somehow?

Bridgette Beato: No, we were unable to be a part of that bid due to the policy requirements, because the agency would not work with us.

Paul Comfort: Okay, so now let's zoom out for a minute, because I'd love to get your perspective as someone who brings 15 years experience operating a DBE now. What's something in the way the DBE Program is implemented, if you had the chance to say "Here's how it **should** be done," what do you say?

Bridgette Beato: Wow, that's a big question, let me think. I guess I'd say from my perspective, the central irony of the DBE program is that it's intended to give these marginalized players more equity in the industry, and yet in some ways, the Program itself kind of marginalizes them. It situates them on the margins of a process designed to de-marginalize them!

Paul Comfort: Please elaborate.

Bridgette Beato: So what I mean by that is, DBEs don't necessarily have a lot of contact with the agencies themselves. They're not generally there at the table when the agency is deciding, well, what percentage set-aside should there be on a given project...

So, first off, if it's a really small percentage that's so incidental it can just become kind of a checkbox thing, right? The prime finds a DBE, but the DBE's actual contributions to the project are minimal to non-existent. From the prime's perspective, it's basically seen as a cost of doing business. They're not expecting or even wanting the DBE to contribute real value to the project. Instead, they just want to be able to say, "You asked for a DBE, we got you a DBE." And if the set-aside in question is small enough, they can do that. It's just a cost of doing business.

Paul Comfort: So how do you solve for that?

Bridgette Beato: To solve for that, you need to give DBEs a bigger percentage of projects. 20 percent. 25 percent. That's how you, as a small business, end up getting real equity in a project. That's when you'll make enough on the project that you've got capital to grow, that you get on a path to becoming a larger entity over time, with more capabilities. Instead of just always existing as this small player operating on the margins who's always just one or two setbacks or unexpected challenges away from extinction.

But even when these larger set-asides exist — and to give credit where credit is due, we are seeing more projects with set-asides like these, and that's a good development – they're still just "goals," not requirements.

And that's our reality, that's not going to change anytime soon. But I still think there's a structural weakness in play when it's the prime who's driving the decision-making process about whether or not a DBE is qualified to do the work in question.

In other words, it's just too easy in the current system to say, "We looked. We made a good-faith effort. But we couldn't find anyone!" And yes, the agency working with the prime has the power to review the prime's decision-making process, and hold them accountable if they feel it wasn't a legitimate effort.

But ultimately I think that spreads out the accountability too much. Because first of all, the agency might choose ***not*** review to the prime's decision. They might just say, "Okay, thanks for trying." Or it might review the decision, but in a really cursory way. As long as the prime has some minimum level of paperwork justifying its decision, the agency says, "Okay, that works!"

So in a lot of situations, it can function as a form of passing the buck. In my opinion, at least in some percentage of projects, the agencies themselves should be charged with making the good-faith effort to find qualified DBEs. Because at the end of the day, it's the DOT's program. It's their baby. So put more of the responsibility for ensuring the Program's goals are actually met on them.

And what that basically means is you let DBEs bid directly on portions of projects, the same way that primes do. Because as long as everything always goes through a prime, as long as the only way a DBE can work on one of these projects is they're a subcontractor to a prime, they're by definition marginalized. You haven't given them a seat at the table where they're acting in truly autonomous fashion.

But if you do let them bid directly, then (a) they're already less marginal than they are under the current system and (b) some of the responsibility for ensuring the Program's success shifts back to the agency, where it should be.

I mean, I'm sure there would be cases where the agency would also say, "Hey, we looked! But we couldn't find a qualified DBE." But I think there'd be fewer of these cases, because the agencies are always going to have more incentive than primes to make true good-faith efforts to find DBEs, because that's the goal of their program.

Paul Comfort: Great. That's an important perspective to be aware of and an interesting proposal to change how our industry operates.

Bridgette Beato: It's a big ask!

Paul Comfort: Well, the idea is out there. That's a start.

Bridgette Beato: Yes.

Paul Comfort: So back to a more nuts-and-bolts question, when it comes to bidding as a subcontractor with a larger company, one of these big A&E firms, how does that work for a small business trying to get in? How do you build a relationship with the primary contractor, and prove that you're capable of doing whatever they'll be bringing you on to do?

Bridgette Beato: I think what you're asking here, at least in part is, "So is having the DBE, the certification, a magic ticket?" And as you probably gather through a lot of the things I've said so far, the answer is definitely, "No, it's not!"

Because, again, the set-asides on these projects are "goals," not mandatory quotas. So a goal can get us in the door, but we still have to make the case to the primary that "Yes, we do have the capabilities," and even better, "Yes, we do have the experience. Here are three examples of projects we've completed that are relevant to what you're need on this project."

Which, obviously, that second part is hard to do when you're just starting out. Often impossible, in fact. So when you are just starting out, it may be that you really do need to focus on relationship-building, and gaining trust with a prime, that you do have the capabilities to successfully complete the project.

Paul Comfort: And what role do you play in the negotiations with the agency?

Bridgette Beato: Honestly, a minimal one. Even when you've gotten to the point where we are, where we do have a long track record of success working on a wide range of projects. The reality is that the way these projects are structured, the primes control that part of the process, they're the ones talking with the agencies, and they like to keep all that very close to the vest.

So as a sub-contractor, at least as things stand now, our customer is very much the prime, not the agency. That's who we're trying to show that we can contribute and really provide value to their proposal to the agency and ultimately to the project itself.

Paul Comfort: Does the prime expect you to staff up ahead of time for these projects? Or do you wait? In other words, if the prime hasn't gotten the contract yet, do they still expect you to operate as if it's a done deal, so that if they do get it, everything's ready to go? Or is it more that you wait until the agency awards the contract to the prime, and then you sign a contract with the prime and start to staff up?

Bridgette Beato: A lot of the time, you're actually expected to have key team leads. Ahead of the deal. Because part of the proposal the prime is making is going to include org charts, and some of those spots on the org chart are people that you, as the sub-contractor, will be supplying. So, yes, you do need to be staffed up in advance, these are actual people who will be fulfilling specific roles on the project. The prime is going to want to include their resumes, their qualifications, because that's a part of how their proposal is being evaluated by the agency. And it may be that these people end up participating in oral interviews with the agency, or other kinds of evaluations that may be part of the agency's review and selection process.

Paul Comfort: Interesting. So what else could our industry be doing in terms of promoting equity and inclusion in public transport?

Bridgette Beato: It's like I said earlier. In my opinion, the really big opportunity involves looking for more ways to facilitate direct contact between DBEs and the agencies.

Because frankly we could make progress on these fronts much faster if we had opportunities to communicate directly with the agencies. That way, we'd get to share our experiences about how projects play out. We get to explain the challenges that result from the current way of doing things, and the kinds of modifications that could make things better....

Now, just to be clear, there are a lot of agencies that do function like true advocates for us and other DBEs. Where if I'm part of proposal, I get immediate follow-up from them, where they're asking questions like "How was this experience for you? Are the primes paying you on time? Are they giving you the work that they said that they were going to give you? Are they giving you the ability to grow your staff and increase the capabilities of your company?"

In other words, are they treating the DBE goal like a requirement to check off with as little engagement and friction as possible? Or are they actually invested in the idea of making the industry more diverse and inclusive, which is in fact the state goal of the DBE program?

And again, I'm a big believer that modernizing our industry in this way is something that benefits everyone in the ecosystem – the primes, sub-contractors like us, the agencies themselves, and obviously public transit users. Because the industry **needs** new ideas. It **needs** innovation. It needs to make more effective on-ramps to the industry for new players, to avoid stagnation and the belief that, well, heck, the status quo has worked okay in the past, so it'll keep working in the future.

When you're looking at it like that, then sure, the primes do have **some** incentive to make the DBE program work as intended. But the major stakeholders that really have the most incentive to make the program work are the agencies themselves. And that's why we need to structurally build in parts of the process where there is direct contact between DBEs and the agencies, and not just rely on the fact that, yes, some agencies understand and act on the spirit of the law, not just the letter of the law. Because if we really want to drive change at the pace it needs to be happening, we need a lot more agencies fully invested in helping DBEs achieve long-term success.

Paul Comfort: Obviously, at this point, you've been immersed in the industry for a while now – 15 years. What advice do you have for a woman or minority who wants to start a business and enter the industry in 2022? What are the first steps they should take to maximize their chances for success?

Bridgette Beato: I think especially if you're just stepping into the industry cold, with no prior experience in it as an employee or a consultant, then do your research. Know exactly what you're getting into. Because like I've said already, a DBE certification doesn't ensure you're going to get part of a contract. I think some people assume, "Okay, these primaries need *someone* to give that set-aside to, so I'll be that someone. And they'll do the heavy lifting as I get up to speed." But that's not really how it works. The primes don't have to choose a DBE to win a project.

Or maybe it just takes a lot longer than you thought it would to get part of a contract, even with your DBE. As we've touched on already, our industry does not have a short turnaround time for awarding work. So if you come in and you only have a few people on your payroll, okay, that's still a few people that you might have to pay for two years before you actually book any business.

So you need to have a very realistic understanding of how the industry works, and more specifically, what your pipeline will look like. Do you have some relationships you'll be able to draw upon? Are you starting completely from scratch? And maybe a little more nuanced – even if you have worked in the industry already, as a consultant or a team lead or whatever, are you also prepared to take on all the new challenges of running your own company? Because now you're going to have a lot more hats to wear. Along with delivering the work on whatever projects you get, you're going to be trying to grow your business.

So a lot of research, enough to get you where you can say, "Okay, here's my plan if things go reasonably well. Here's my plan if things go terribly. And here's my plan for when things start going wrong, even when it seemed like everything was going right."

And definitely part of that research, and just your planning in general, is how are you going to be drawing on any relationships with people and advocates in the industry that you're bringing to the game. What's your plan to strengthen those relationships? Who are existing players in the industry who you don't know yet, but could realistically become a partner or advocate for you? Because even having just one strong relationship like that can really make a big difference to your chances, especially when you're just starting out.

Paul Comfort: Okay, so switching gears a little bit, tell us more about how the certification process. It happens on a state-by-state level, right?

Bridgette Beato: It does. So, for example, I'm certified in 39 states as a DBE. There are a lot of other similar certifications as well – SBEs, or small business enterprises. WBEs, or woman-owned businesses. And sub-certifications for more localized use – LDBEs, LSBEs. Basically, these variations give the agencies more flexibility to pursue even more specific goals, so that's why they exist. And if you want to make sure you're maximizing your potential options, you try to get as many of these that are applicable.

Paul Comfort: Got it.

Bridgette Beato: And just to elaborate – the standards are set on the federal level. The FTA defines what a DBE is. But you still have to get certified in any state you actually want to do business in. So you start by going through the certification process in your home state, and that's a process that includes completing a lot of paperwork and providing different kinds of documentation. And then you also go through a series of interviews with people from your state's DOT. The WBE, SBE and many others are performed at a state level, within the bands of their requirements. So you have to be aware of a lot of different rules and regulations.

Once you get that initial certification in your home state, you can use it to expand into other states. And basically the process varies. Some states require you to go through additional interviews or ask for on-site visits.

Even in the best cases, it's a rigorous process. And it can take a lot of time and back-and-forth, especially these days because COVID has created backlogs at the state agencies. Also, this isn't a one-time thing. You actually have to renew your certifications every year. So at Lumenor, we now have a full-time staff person where that's basically their job, obtaining and maintaining these certifications, because we're now certified in so many states.

Paul Comfort: Let me ask you about cash flow too, because I've heard from a lot of small businesses that the turnaround time for them to get paid after they do the work can be lengthy.

Bridgette Beato: When you're a subcontractor, what happens is the prime bills the agency, the agency pays the prime, and then the prime pays you.

Paul Comfort: So how does that impact average turnaround time for payments to you?

Bridgette Beato: Realistically, a minimum turnaround time is 90 days. But that's only when things are going smoothly. In most cases, you'll be submitting invoices to the prime on a monthly basis, but then they've got to submit their own invoice to the agency, the agency has to process that invoice, et cetera.

And if the agency returns the invoice to the prime for any reason – they've got questions about what's being billed for, for example – then that's going to start the cycle again. The prime has to submit a new invoice, the agency has to process it. So obviously, you, as subcontractor, are definitely the last to get paid on the job, and ultimately dependent on the efficiency of the other parties involved in the process.

And here's, for example, one way that dependency can play out: You might be in a phase of the project where you're working a lot of hours, but the prime isn't. So it doesn't have a whole lot of incentive to submit an invoice until it has more hours to bill. In a scenario like that, you might end up not getting paid until, say, August, for work you actually did in January. So it's something you've got to stay extremely on top of, in terms of the assumptions you're making about cash flow and your overall business.

Especially if you're new to the business. This is an example of what I was referring to earlier – what's your plan for when things start going wrong, even when things seemed like they were going right? You got this contract. You completed your work. And still no cash flow. So what do you do now?

Because in reality, things like this are going to happen. There's going to be delays. There's going to be postponements, in all parts of the process. I mean, just one example, I remember a project I worked on, the prime would submit a package invoice that included all their sub-contractors – and there was a lot of them on this particular project.

And if there was even just one line item off, the agency would immediately kick it back to prime for correction, even if the amount in question was tiny. Literally, like 25 cents off. Then, the prime would correct the error, send it back, and the agency would find another error or discrepancy somewhere, and it'd go back again! And eventually nine months had passed!

Another issue is how retainage works from a subcontractor's perspective, right? It's pretty standard practice on most of these jobs to have a retainage clause in play – the agency retains some amount of their payment to the prime until everything's completed. But if the contractor's allowed to pass that down to subcontractors, that can become really untenable because of the duration of some of these projects. I was on a project once where it was literally a five-year process. I completed my work in the first year, and then had to wait four more years for the prime to pay me for the final 10% of the work.

Paul Comfort: That's a long time to wait.

Bridgette Beato: When you're a small business, it can be catastrophic. The DBE Program does have "prompt payment" policies – but that only applies to when they actually release the retainage to a contractor. In other words, when an agency releases retainage to a prime, and the subcontractor is owed some portion of that money, the prime has 30 days to pay the subcontractor. But if the deal is structured so that prime isn't getting any payment until everything's completed, that 30 days doesn't really make a difference. As the subcontractor, sure, better 30 days than 60 days. But I've already waited multiple years to get paid before a payment even starts getting considered as "late."

Paul Comfort: What about performance bonds and bid bonds – you know, other kinds of insurance that an agency might require from a contractor to cover any failures to complete the contracted work as specified. Are those hurdles as well?

Bridgette Beato: So far, at least, that hasn't been an issue for us. When we've been in situations where that's something the agency is asking for, they want us to hold those bonds, we've been lucky to be working with primes who've told the agency that they, as the larger firm in the deal, should really be doing that.

And I chalk that up to growing awareness in the industry overall, about what kinds of things it can be doing to really support DBEs and the goals underlying the DBE program, and that's a great example of that.

Paul Comfort: Well, great. That's good to hear. Now in terms of moving forward, you're also on the board of WTS. Tell us about that and the role that they're playing in helping women move ahead in the public transit.

Bridgette Beato: Absolutely. WTS International is a trade organization whose mission is advancing and promoting women in the transportation as a means toward increasing the industry's role as a vital public good. So a lot of what we do involves outreach to get more women interested and involved in the industry, and then also a lot of support for women who are participating in the industry. This includes scholarships, seminars, and various other kinds of training and educational opportunities. And overall, the goal is not just to bring women into the industry, but to help them rise to leadership positions and career advancement opportunities that give them real equity in the system. Which in turns is going to make the system more innovative, adaptive, and responsive to the communities it serves.

Paul Comfort: Great. Well, we've covered a lot, but is there anything else you'd like to share about promoting equity and inclusion in public transportation, or advice for small businesses that want to break into the industry as a contractor?

Bridgette Beato: I think I would just reiterate one last time that this call for greater diversity — with real equity behind that diversity — should be viewed first and foremost as an opportunity to modernize our industry in ways that will improve conditions for all the players in the ecosystem. Because as we bring in new players, we're bringing in fresh perspectives, more innovation, and just, you know, the dynamism we need to keep public transport relevant as our users have new expectations, new needs, other options they can choose.

In the end, public transportation is a public good, so that means the industry itself should be just as diverse as the different publics we're building these systems for. And the way you achieve that diversity and inclusion within our industry is to give DBEs more ambitious ways to participate in these projects, including opportunities to work directly with state and federal agencies.

Which, fortunately, is something we're starting to see more of. Like if it's a contract for less than $5 million, a DBE can bid on it as prime contractor, instead of just functioning as a sub-contractor.

So this is similar to what I was talking about earlier, this idea of building in more opportunities for DBEs to work directly with the agencies. I'm thinking in particular of the Port Authority of NY & NJ, and how they're managing some of their "bench" contracts now.

Now, I guess first I should explain what a bench contract is. It's basically a basically a 3 to 5 year contract for a huge range of services, where a number of firms that have been selected for the contract can bid on specific "task orders" when they arise.

Paul Comfort: They're the bench that gets to play in this game.

Bridgette Beato: Yes. And typically, if you're a DBE, you're not going to be one of the players. You might be a sub-contractor to a Prime who's on the bench, but even if they end winning some of the task orders, there's no guarantee they'll sub-contract any of that out to you.

Paul Comfort: You stay on the bench.

Bridgette Beato: Trust me, I've been on contracts where I'm sub-contractor to someone on the bench, and the entire five years passes without a dollar of revenue coming to us.

Paul Comfort: And how is the Port Authority of NY & NJ changing that?

Bridgette Beato: They're letting small firms submit a proposal at any time during the duration of the bench project. And if you possess the qualifications for any subject area, you're added to the bench. So when they put out task orders for $5 million or less, you'll get them directly and can compete for them against everyone else. If you win it, you work directly with the agency as the prime on that project.

Paul Comfort: So just what you're saying our industry really needs more of.

Bridgette Beato: Yeah, I'd love to see this approach really start to spread and become the norm. There's still no guarantee that we do get the business – we have to compete. But we get to interface directly with the agency, and that makes such a big difference.

Paul Comfort: That's great, and I think probably a good place to wrap this up. So, thanks, Bridgette. And we wish you continued success in your company as you continue to grow. And thanks for being part of our book.

Bridgette Beato: Thank you, Paul. This is a great topic and I'm glad you're bringing it forward.

JACOBS

Freddie Fuller, *VP & COMTO Immediate Past National Chair,*
Sabrina Becker, *Global Director, Inclusion and Diversity,*
Denise LaMaison-Bell, *Jacobs Black Employee Network,*
Phil LaCombe, *Senior Transportation Planner*

Jacobs has been working....

Paul Comfort: Would you like to describe what Jacobs is as a company and then kick us off on what you're doing in this field of equity and inclusion?

Sabrina Becker: Absolutely. So I think what's important to know is that Jacobs has a long history of getting Inclusion and Diversity (I and D) to be a core part of our business.

Anything you read on the core business of Jacobs - you'll see engineering, you'll see technology, you'll see cyber, but you'll see that I and D runs through all of that. And we've had a really fantastic journey the last five years, from a place of understanding we had work to do, to getting to where we are five years from now. Which is, I don't think the I and D journey is ever complete, but we certainly have been trying to lead the way and not wait for someone to tell us what to do.

But instead, we engage with our communities, engage with our clients, engage with our own employees. Especially this group that you have here is fantastic. And I can tell you some great stories about that and how do we begin to integrate and then to tie all of those goals back into actual business goals, to tie that back into compensation, to tie that back into measurable promises that we can put out to our stakeholders, our board, our employees, and then follow through with those promises.

So I'll stop there. Cause I don't want to get too far. I could talk about this for an hour, but that's the beginning of where I think it's important to understand that Jacobs has been on a journey, continues to be on a journey and it's all about connecting people and an understanding from the ground up, what we need to be doing as a company to make a difference.

Paul Comfort: That's great. Freddie, can you give us context for who Jacobs is. as a company.

Freddie Fuller : Well, you know, Jacobs is a global architecture and engineering firm that is quickly transforming itself into more of a solutions company.

We have about 56,000 employees with 400 offices in 40 countries. And obviously we do all kinds of work. I jokingly tell people all the time. I won't say that we don't do it because we probably touch it in some way, whether it's a commercial client, whether it's a federal, state or local government, there's probably some Jacobs engagement. Whether it's an infrastructure project, whether it's health care, whether it's science and technology. Jacobs is large. One of the largest contractors a space exploration client has is Jacobs. So, we stretch far and wide. It is really about transforming a company to be a solutions provider dealing with things like climate change and cyber, areas that are taking the world by storm.

Paul Comfort: That's great. Denise, tell us some about what you've been doing in this area and what your plans are and why.

Denise LaMaison-Bell : Yeah. Thank you, Paul.

My colleagues mentioned a couple of words as they were answering, responding to you. Connectivity, engagement, journey, relationship. This is what it's all about, right? We at Jacobs, we're good at the business. We're outstanding at the business.

This Diversity, Equity and Inclusion (DEI) work, this work is about people, right? It's at the core of it. So, it's not a race. It's not, it's, it's a journey. It's a continuing. Building a relationship, it's a continual building of trust and authenticity. We are about building up the people through the organization so that we can do all these plays that my colleagues have just mentioned.

It's at the core of it. The businesses are the people. If the people are happy, your business is going to thrive. And so that's what we do here at Jacobs is concentrate and focus on that with this DEI work that we do.

Paul Comfort: That's great. Tell me some specifically about some of the programs you have going there at Jacobs.

Denise LaMaison-Bell : So specifically we have eight outstanding employee networks. We're all in the umbrella of what you see there together.

So these groups help us to increase that connectivity and engagement with our workforce throughout the organization. At various levels, whether it be community outreach and volunteerism there and involving our clients in that aspect or learning and development opportunities, professional development, growth opportunities for our workforce. So that they can continue to grow in their journey and thrive in their careers and also show their value, add to the business in other ways. Like start a Black History Month celebration. We do an international Women's Month. So all these things and celebration of who we are as people contribute to outstanding success as an organization.

Paul Comfort: Great. Phillip they mentioned that you did a study at transit client in Maryland. Tell me about your role there and what you found in your study.

Phil LaCombe: I've been a transportation planner with Jacobs for over five years now. And this Maryland client has been my main client during my work for Jacobs. And during the early pandemic days our Maryland client identified that they needed to take a strategic look at the agency and come up with a plan for the future.

That took into account the very fast changing world we're in and they saw some of the trends that you'd mentioned about essential workers not getting necessary service and the conversation about the movement for black lives and various equity focused initiatives and topics of concern around the country and they wanted to do an equity centered strategic plan.

So we put together for them this plan that makes a series of commitments based around different themes and at the center of those themes is equity. So we looked at traditional things like physical access, of course. But also looking beyond that to people and resources to diversifying leadership, the employees and employee culture and being a diverse and inclusive place.

Then on the resources we looked at prioritizing equity in the service planning process. And then in capital budgeting as well, taking into account data that's readily available about race, ethnicity, income, age, et cetera, to center equity in the capital budgeting process too. So we worked with them to create this plan and we're working on the implementation of the plan right now.

In general, what we found through the planning process and what I think many transit agencies are working on right now is that the tools that transit agencies were given by the Civil Rights Act of 1964 are great. And it prevented a lot of potential harm, additional harm to historically disadvantaged communities, but they're just not enough to achieve equity. You might be able to get some sense of equality from them, but equity is not really achievable with just those things.

So in our role as consultants at Jacobs, one of the big things we're doing is finding those best practices across the United States for equity in transit planning, transit service, transit culture and helping our clients move towards some of those best practices. Then expanding upon them so that they can be the leaders and then they can share and keep building upon this because transit service is run by public agencies and public agencies need to be cautious at times, right?

So our job is, we can kind of push them a little bit and say, someone's done this. You could build upon it. You know, there's a precedent here and keep moving the needle.

Paul Comfort: Would you be able to give me a few of what those practices are that you've identified that other transit agencies are doing successfully?

Phil LaCombe: Yes, so one of them is transit client in Northern California. They have a service equity policy that mandates a strategy to identify projects that would make service equal or better in specific targeted equity neighborhoods. So capital projects, service improvements, et cetera.

Another one is a large transit client in Southern California who has a transit equity score that they use to define areas, specific areas of need. And then they use that throughout their planning process.

The example that we pulled and really helps our Maryland client and we're working on adopting right now is actually from the a transit client in Boston and when they were having difficult budget constraints. During the worst of the pandemic, they created this tool, it's basically a two axis chart.

You've got ridership on one side and then what they call transit critical populations on the other. So demographics. What they wanted to do was prioritize, restoring routes and expanding service for lines that serve the most people. The ridership was strong even during the pandemic, indicating that those essential worker populations are using those services.

And then they looked at the demographics of the people that are served by that route or train line. Are they historically disadvantaged populations? So thinking about the service and how to allocate service on this two axis chart, you know, it's not that complicated, the data is all there. It's a framework.

It's a way of thinking. Right? That's one of the tools we've helped our Maryland client with and are helping them adopt right now.

Paul Comfort: Thank you. Now Freddie, can you give me a view of where we're at right now in 2022 nationally on this whole area of equity inclusion in public transportation? And then can you address what's the role of COMTO (as the Immediate Past Chair) in helping this effort?

Freddie Fuller : First of all, looking at it nationally, I think we have a couple of lines of activity going on. We have a lot of folks that are kind of just waking up to this equity and inclusion space, this DEI space, if you will. Some folks haven't always been on board with it, or haven't been really out in front with it, there hasn't been a lot of visibility around it. It's kind of been one of those things that people don't talk about. So you've got that group, then you've got another group of folks that have been intentional from day one and they are always there you know, towing the line, carrying the message.

And I'll give you a quick example. I won't name the agency, but we had an agency just last week ask us in-depth questions about what does our leadership team look like? How diverse are we? How many minorities are on the leadership team? How many women are on the leadership team? What does that board of directors look like?

This was all part of their procurement process. Now they wanted to know what action steps have we put into place. And I think that's a best practice that you've got to see a lot of other transit agencies start to use. And to speak to COMTO (Conference of Minority Transportation Officials) - COMTO has been the voice of equity for transportation for 50 plus years.

Now it's not new to COMTO. You know, this is the cool thing to do now. People are making statements. But you have to remember, this has been a challenge for a very long time. And we have been about leveling the playing field and opening doors, not only in public transportation, but in all modes of transportation.

That's why I tell people COMTO still has a place and still has a relevant voice. As long as we have firsts that continue to be had, there's still a need for COMTO. As long as we have people trying to understand why is this important? Or they're asking the question, why is there this emphasis, there's still a need for COMTO. There's going to be a need as long as people don't understand and don't get it.

So this agency is asking questions and other agencies around the country are starting to. It's not about them being aggressive. It's about being intentional about equity and inclusion. And this is what intentionality looks like when you're intentional. And you're asking these questions. This is the reality of what it's like. This is not extra. Don't look at this as something hard to do, look at it as the right thing to do.

And for a long time, we haven't done the right thing and it's time to do the right thing.

Paul Comfort: Thank you. Sabrina please provide us some more specifics about what Jacobs is doing so that other companies can look and say, oh, these are good examples.

Sabrina Becker: I want to echo what Freddie said that this is a movement that is gaining traction. We're seeing more and more clients move towards this. We're seeing more and more clients ask us, what is your diversity? What, what are you really doing? What are the percentages of your board of your leaders? And absolutely, that's something that we're very proud to be on the forefront of a number of things that we're doing.

I would love Denise, if you can talk a little bit about our action plan for equality and justice. So I'll leave that one to you. It's an amazing program. It is a key of what we're doing. A few other additional things I would love to mention. We are looking internally to make sure that we have equity across the boards on gender equality.

We're looking at who's where, not just do we have a number, but are those numbers in the right places? So if we're increasing our number of women, we have a 40, 40, 20 goal. And if we're increasing the number of women, are we increasing that across the board? Is there a pipeline that is in place to make sure that we have people who can move into these positions?

And yes, we have great executive diversity right now. Do we have the right pipeline to succeed that and continue to make this the way Jacobs lives every day, not just meeting the number that we challenged ourselves to meet? We're also incredibly proud of our employee networks. We have so much input from these large groups that we have over 20,000 of our 55,000 employees involved in these employee networks.

And I'll also say we have a very strong social value and equity practice that is really cutting edge leading the way to make sure that we have the experts on board who can come in and advise clients.

Phil LaCombe: And like Freddie said, it's maybe brand new to them. This may be something they're struggling to kick off and we have put the infrastructure together.

You know, we're not just going to take the journey with you where we know what you're going to experience. We want to be there right by your side to make sure that we can help you along the way. And so diversity, inclusion. Absolutely. But that, that equity piece is really key as well and looking at models to do that, not just saying the right thing to do, but how do we actually take the science to it and look at it and help you study it?

Talking to our employees, talking to our clients and continually listening so that we can push forward the needle and dedicating ourselves, measuring ourselves and holding ourselves accountable to our goals.

The same as we do say our financial goals, it's just key that everybody understands this as part of who we are. So you said this was going to be in the hands of executives. Our executives have been fantastic at saying we are going to put our money where our mouth is, and we are going to follow these policies.

We are going to implement these practices and we're going to hold ourselves to.

Denise LaMaison-Bell : So Freddie talked about the opportunity for us to get it right. Right? So our action plan for advancing justice and equality allows us to do just that and continue to build upon the existing culture that we have, a global culture of inclusion and diversity. The strategies yes but it also allowed us to put some actionable initiatives.

You know, we had a lot of dialogue last year and dwelled in 2020 and continued through 2021. But then how do we take that dialogue? Move it from dialogue to sustainable action. And so the action plan for advancing justice and equality, something born out of our black employee network to fruition.

And so it really highlights amplifying our culture of belonging. We are recruiting, retaining and advancing black employees based on merit. And then, you know, as Sabrina was talking about earlier, our contribution to structural change in the broader society. And so having these three pillars that we're focused on and we're able to hone in on really gives us the template for our journey, right?

As we move forward in this culture of diversity, equity and inclusion, not only here at Jacobs, but like you said, in helping others get to a point where they can do this as well.

Paul Comfort: Excellent. And Freddie, I was hoping you could tell me about your CEO and his commitment to this. You were mentioning that to me on our pre-call.

Freddie Fuller : Absolutely. Steve Demetriou has led from the front since day one. He became the CEO of Jacobs in 2015, and he came in the door with this message. And not only talking it but walking it. Steve's an executive sponsor of Jacob's women's network and our black employee network. He's gone on to see change and implement change. I mean from gender equity at the highest levels of leadership to being intentional about hiring leaders of color.

And certainly there's a groundswell from the grassroots level employees that are leading the way as a result of the message that he's put out to us. The key with it is we stick with the messaging. We stick with the actions that we continue to deliver. We have these continuous conversations - what we call courageous conversation.

And we've had hundreds of courageous conversations evolve in all levels of employees at Jacobs. And these calls have allowed people to express how they feel, to talk about what it's like in the workplace, the discrimination, or even the racism that they've experienced and to literally share what has happened.

Uh, people have cried on these calls. People have really broken down and we've addressed all sorts of topics. When we've had these courageous conversations and these courageous conversations continue, it wasn't something that we just did at the spirit of moment. It's something where we've opened the door to allow people to talk about things that we don't traditionally talk about at work, but bring these things into the workplace because most of our life is spent here and we need to face some of the realities and not continue to sweep things under the rug.

We've really had to get comfortable with the uncomfortable, and that's what I challenge our industry to do is to get comfortable with the uncomfortable. You can't change anything that isn't faced.

And you've got to remember that. As long as you continue to not talk about it, it is going to continue to perpetuate itself and not until you start to face it and do something will there be real change

Denise LaMaison-Bell : Oh, if I could just add something too, because the important thing that people have to remember is that this is something that's honorable.

You know, Freddie mentioned that it's, you know, a lot of folks are doing it now because it sounds good. You get the good sound bite, you get the good tagline, but these are the issues. When it comes to DEI work, you are impacting somebody's life - an individual's life. And you have to understand that this is an everyday walk, so it has to be an everyday talk.

It has to be embedded into an organization. It can't be an afterthought. It can't be something you just do to get the spotlight, but it has to really be a part of your organization. It can't be the first thing to get cut. You know, when it comes to budgets and funding, it has to be woven in so that it's a culture building moment and opportunity.

Paul Comfort: Thank you, Phil, were you going to add something else?

Phil LaCombe: Yeah, it's something I've found meaningful and something I really like about being with Jacobs is that we have an annual priority setting process for all employees, leaders, everyone.

And as part of that, we've built diversity equity inclusion right into it. So it's my understanding that basically all the leaders, people, managers at all levels need to be setting priorities, and that includes equity and inclusion. Everyone is strongly suggested, right down to the associate level to include equity and inclusion in their priorities.

SUMMARY

TERRY WHITE

Chief Executive Officer
King County Metro
(Seattle, Washington)

In conclusion...

As transit leaders, we are entrusted with advancing a human right: the freedom to move. We connect people to community, education, entertainment, family, friends, jobs, medical care, museums, parks, shopping and more. We strive to make getting where you want to go accessible, affordable, reliable, safe, seamless and stress-free.

Transit is finally receiving the national attention it deserves because of the belated realization that the movement we make possible is the connective tissue upon which everything else depends. Businesses can't fill job vacancies if people aren't able to get to work. A person can't attend school or receive vocational training without a way to get there. And health care relies on reliable transportation for medical professionals and patients alike.

Our charge as transit agencies must be to expand even further in the years ahead. Although our transit systems—and the cities, counties, and towns we serve—vary greatly, we are united by three strategic imperatives:

- How to prioritize audiences as we rebuild ridership.
- How to invest in community relations to guide us.
- How to ensure our environmental trajectory delivers a future worth inheriting.

THE NEW DAILY RIDERS

While we don't know exactly what the future looks like, we do know that the car – whether gas or electric – is not the answer. We want to live, work and play in communities marked by greenery, pedestrian paths and birds chirping, not widening highways, parking superstructures and the din of traffic. We need a suite of options – across buses, bicycle lanes, on-demand services, rail and vanpools – that allow people to move freely based on their interests and abilities, rather than endlessly funneling cars into congested travel arteries.

Pre-pandemic trends toward more hybrid and work-from-home positions have increased exponentially since 2020. The result is that the profile of everyday riders has shifted permanently. While most temporary work-from-home roles have since shifted to a hybrid schedule, many individuals will never return to 100% in-person work. Generally, that means fewer riders, fewer fares and potentially less revenue to deliver the frequent, reliable service that customers require.

To rebuild ridership, we must continue to appeal to occasional commuters and invite riders to take transit to a limitless number of non-work destinations. But what's even more important is that we invest resources into building a transit system that is attractive to the prospective customers who are already asking us for a ride. These customers tend to have lower incomes and—due to skyrocketing housing prices and the cost of living—cannot afford to live close to the rail lines and transit corridors that were often built decades ago. These future riders will benefit tremendously from affordable, reliable public transportation to and from opportunities and services.

But expanding service to these underserved customers is not as straightforward as adding a new bus route from neighborhood centers to the downtown core. These future riders live in areas that are less dense and more decentralized. Their frequent destinations are in no one direction. And their desired hours of travel must align with work shifts that can begin before dawn and go late into the night. The good news is that we, as transit agencies, don't need to begin with knowing the answers, but rather to start the community conversations and commit to seeing this work through to fruition.

COMMUNITY IS KING

Transit desperately needs new mobility solutions—especially first- and last-mile approaches for underserved residents—but these solutions won't come from the heads of transit agencies. Not even the direction on which *problems* to prioritize may come from us. Instead, our role is to be facilitators and servant leaders to the communities we serve—and the communities we wish to serve. That takes resources, time and a roadmap that cannot be pre-written, but I promise that the learning and the payoff are worth it.

At King County Metro (Metro), we established a Mobility Equity Cabinet in 2019 to advise us on infrastructure and transit investments, new mobility solutions and how to engage communities in decision-making. We needed the voices of traditionally underrepresented perspectives of priority populations, which we define as people who (1) are Black, Indigenous or of color; (2) have low or no income; (3) have disabilities; and/or (4) are linguistically diverse. Across a number of months, we co-created a set of guiding principles and recommendations for centering equity and sustainability in Metro's policies. Importantly, we paid members for their participation to acknowledge their expertise and time. Along the way, we gathered input from transit riders, the public (especially priority populations), regional partners, stakeholders, elected officials and employees. In 2020, the King County Council adopted the Equity Cabinet's recommendations, called the Equity Framework. Then, in 2021, the Equity Framework and further co-creation work drove changes to Metro's long-range planning documents to ensure that transit investments go where they are needed most. The Council was unanimous in approving these groundbreaking legislative updates.

In addition to agency-wide community advisors, Metro has an ongoing Access Paratransit Advisory Committee. We also regularly convene the Young Members of the Mobility Equity Cabinet. We seek to be in continuous contact with advocates, communities and neighborhoods—especially as we look to add, improve or revise service. When it comes to first- and last-mile solutions, for example, community engagement has guided us toward services that work the best for a specific area. Sometimes, that means Via to Transit, which provides an on-demand car trip between home and a transit hub for the same cost as a bus fare. Other times, a Ride Pingo to Transit van is better equipped to link riders between transit and a worksite.

King County Executive Dow Constantine also directed Metro to co-create with community where the stakes are highest. Following the murder of George Floyd in 2020 and our Executive's acknowledgment of racism as a public health crisis, Metro began working with community members—especially priority populations—and employees to reimagine how to create a safe and welcoming environment on transit. After months of deep engagement, we shared recommended approaches with the King County Council informed by the insights of roughly 8,000 people, focusing on the BIPOC communities disproportionately impacted by inequitable safety and security policies and practices. Then, earlier in 2022, we began implementing pilot programs that respond to our community members' strong desire for a compassionate and visible presence that shows up in the right way.

SUSTAINABILITY

At Metro, we lead with equity, but it's for good reason that our other two core values are safety and sustainability.

Safety is recognizing that the health and wellbeing of our customers and employees are paramount. Our mission is for everyone to get where they need to go in order to thrive, but nothing is more important than being safe and feeling welcome throughout that entire journey. Being a new arrival to this country, living with a disability, your gender identity, your sexual orientation or your ethnicity should not be a barrier to feeling secure when you ride with us. We have similarly high standards within our workplace—while acknowledging what we must do on our system and in our organization's culture. We are fully engaged in both places as we strive to become a "beloved community."

Compared to equity and safety, it can be tempting to delay or demote sustainability—especially when budgets are tight. However, the dire urgency of the climate crisis means we must do even more—and do it faster—to reduce greenhouse gas emissions and direct a culture shift before it's too late. In recent years, King County has seen extreme weather like never before—from reduced rainfall and resulting wildfires to unprecedented snowstorms to weeks of heat in a region that didn't require air conditioning. We know that the continuation of these trends will make all our other aspirations for a brighter, fairer future moot—and that the first to suffer severely will be our neighbors with the least resources and the fewest options.

While transit is already "green," we have an opportunity to do even more to reduce pollution and to encourage technologies—and entire industries—to follow suit. For these reasons, Metro is converting its entire bus fleet—more than 1,400 strong—to zero-emission by the ambitious date of 2035. We have made similar commitments across our other transit modes and support vehicles. Earlier this year, we welcomed the first of our next-generation of 40- and 60- foot battery-electric buses into service, each with the ability to handle every type of terrain and to travel more than 140 miles on a charge.

In the second quarter of 2022, the Federal Transportation Administration (FTA) named Metro the nation's most equitable transit agency in combatting climate change. They credited our agency- and county-wide ambitions and our equity lens. We intentionally prioritized neighborhoods with the worst pollution—which house a disproportionate number of BIPOC and low-income community members—for the new clean-air buses. We also brought the supporting bases and charging stations—and the accompanying family-wage jobs with benefits and a pension—to those areas.

IF YOU WANT TO GO FAR, GO TOGETHER

I've seen how mobility benefits communities, and I've lived it, too. In my more than 30 years in transit, I know we're not simply delivering a more affordable fare, increased frequency of service, a new bus route, translated schedules or an updated wheelchair securement system. Instead, when we improve transit, we expand opportunity.

During my childhood in south King County, transit was my family's only option for getting from a place to a place. We were a family of four—Black, low-income, and raised by our mother, whose disability prevented her from driving.

Even so, my mother provided us with opportunities that would brighten our future. To get to those opportunities, we used transit. Those journeys took us to places in life far beyond what we could have ever imagined.

Some of those destinations included the schools in Seattle where I'd earn college admission. When I earned my degree, I knew exactly where I wanted to work and applied for every Metro job opening in the newspaper. I served in 14 positions before becoming General Manager.

To this day, transit is where I work, read, rest and reminisce. And whether it's bus or rail, I still enjoy riding to a place. But place is never just a physical address. Place is socio-economic. Place is one's position within society. Place is a specific condition. Place is a state of mind.

Growing up, our family's ability to move by way of the transit system was life changing. Unfortunately, movement through the transit system was not always straightforward and efficient. My childhood transit system was not designed with input from family units of poor, Black, disability-challenged dreamers. Nor did the system intentionally look out for English-language learners and foreign-born dreamers. Still, transit helped to move this 10-year-old dreamer to a better place.

Imagine if transit had intentionally included the voices of historically marginalized and silenced communities in the planning process! What place would that bring us to—both personally and in our region? Guided by our communities, that imagined place is precisely where King County Metro is going.

I invite every transit agency to join us on this journey and to work together along the way.